KOLKATA

For my daughters Sureya and Anoushka,
I hope you use this book as a tool to
continue our family legacy.

KOLKATA

RECIPES FROM THE HEART OF BENGAL

RINKU DUTT

Smith Street Books

Contents

Introduction

Kolkata – city of culture and of evocative food – there is no place like it. The city, formerly known as Calcutta when under colonial rule, is the capital of West Bengal and is located on the eastern bank of the River Hooghly. The river port is the oldest in India and the proximity of the Bay of Bengal means that the markets are always bursting with the freshest fish. I love this city and, in particular, its food. Bengali cuisine is fascinating and, when cooked right, I find it the most satisfying to eat. It is very different to the food made in other regions of India, and one that I think really should be introduced to more people around the world, which is why I have written this book.

As one of India's most populous cities, to be in Kolkata is to feel the hustle and bustle completely surround you. Loud horns constantly beep on the street for no other reason than that they are a part of the vehicles and there to be used (one taxi driver told me this when I asked why he hit the horn every ten seconds)! Despite this, the general attitude to life is laid back – everything can and will be done. The reputation of the city as a cultural hub (Kolkata is considered the birthplace of modern Indian literary and artistic thought) persists and means that a love of conversation, for politics, for traditional music and styles of dress is still very much alive. The architecture may be damp and deteriorating, but it is all so vibrant with colour. The bells ringing in the temples, worshippers seeking their blessings from the goddesses, the fragrance of incense sticks burning, smelling the aromas of food being cooked in the houses as you walk by, the balconies, the crumbling paint, the rickshaws, autos and yellow taxis ... all make the city such a treasure and I have always felt grateful to be part of it through my family roots and connections.

Although I grew up in the UK, as a child of Bengali parents I was never allowed to forget my heritage. My father, Ranadeb (Ron), was born in Kolkata, but left India in the 1970s, meeting my mother, Rita, and steadily building a life

in London. Our happy family of four, including myself and my sister, Ria, were brought up to honour our roots. My grandparents were settled in Kolkata and we visited regularly. Every year, my parents made a point of returning to India so that we could meet our grandparents and relatives, and so the connection with our motherland never faded.

We grew up eating Bengali food and even at home my parents would speak to us in the mother tongue and introduce us to various traditional art forms. Learning *Rabindra Sangeet* (the songs of Tagore), Tagorean dance and various other classical dance forms was an integral part of my upbringing and that is how I became so attached to Bengali culture and lifestyle.

From the time I was little, food was given a lot of importance at home. It is a known fact that Bengalis are big foodies. Food is key to our lifestyle and conversations often revolve around it. The love for cooking food, eating food and talking about food is a cycle that plays out on repeat in nearly every Bengali household. And the more I discovered about the variety in Bengali cuisine, the more I became fascinated by it. What I loved most was the way my parents introduced us to a new dish almost every weekend. From fish-head curry (*muri ghonto*) to lentil cakes served in a rich tomato sauce (*dokar dalna*), this food was unique and offered us the most interesting textures and flavours. As we sat down together, relishing those dishes inspired by my grandmother's age-old recipes, we were told family stories and traditional tales that would make the dishes all the more special. They would make their way straight to our hearts – and, as we all know, the stomach and the heart are eternally connected!

An affinity for food and feeding other people is a family passion I have inherited. These roots go back to my great-grandfather, who opened a restaurant in Kolkata called Central Hotel. Later, the restaurant changed its name to Amber. Amber is considered a part of 'Old Kolkata' and is famous for its sumptuous food, especially the kebabs. I have always been inspired by this story and proud of my foodie heritage.

Several years ago, I spent three years living and working in Kolkata and fell in love with the city. When you live somewhere, you naturally attune yourself to

daily life and the pulse of a place, and with every passing day your connection to it grows stronger. The heady combination of streets crowded with people, traffic and heritage fascinated me. I loved listening to the radio on the famous yellow cab rides, the tropical climate and, most importantly, the variety of fantastic street food. In fact, I was so inspired by the food that I felt the urge to do something so that I could bring back these unforgettable tastes and flavours to London. This is how my street-food business, Raastawala, was conceived.

Back then, it was just a dream that would not have been anything near to what it is today without the support of my husband Neelan and dad Ron. Raastawala is a family affair and if you visit you cannot miss our family members running around in aprons, adding a dash of love to each and every dish served! The sense of satisfaction we derive from feeding people cannot be described – it's something I learned from my parents. Through Raastawala, I am able to achieve this and it is the greatest feeling when you see someone enjoy and appreciate the food you make. Since Raastawala started about eight years ago, we have organically grown, mainly by word of mouth. We have built a small yet strong community of customers who enjoy our street food and also welcome the supper clubs and tiffin meals we provide. We serve the dishes that I have grown up eating and that my parents have spent their lives cooking.

My interest in collecting and reviving these family recipes has become a journey in itself. Having moved away from the family home, I would visit and spend weekends with my parents, carefully watching them cook these dishes and attempting to write them down. This was actually quite difficult, as so much Indian cooking is done by *andaaj*, which translates to 'estimate'. The food is quite literally cooked by 'measurements of the eye and instinct'. When I asked my parents about this, they would laugh it off and say that's the way they were taught to cook, and sure enough the dishes always turned out the same and were always delicious.

My little notebook of scribbled recipes, with lines crossed out and food stains all over it, began to get fuller and soon I had a book of treasures that held so many hours of hard work, arguments, the frustration of my parents (as I doggedly asked about each step of a recipe), history and beautiful memories. These dishes were the ones I loved to cook and were loved by everyone who ate them. It was then that I realised that writing a cookbook and sharing these recipes would make them accessible to many more people and give the opportunity for food lovers to cook the dishes that had been made in our family for generations, taking them from the small traditional kitchens in Kolkata to ones in other lands.

Like all Indian cuisines, Bengali food has been influenced by the climate, its geographic location and religion to create a unique array of dishes.

In Kolkata, the monsoon season is from June to September. During this time, the air is humid and the temperatures are high, and when the skies finally open, bringing a respite to the heat, heavy rain pours down. This has to be my favourite time of the year, as I find the monsoons romantic and atmospheric (even though they do make practical life rather difficult and uncomfortable). I love to watch the pouring rain, sitting on the swing on the balcony of our second-floor Kolkata flat with a cup of masala tea, watching passers by rush to get under shelter, umbrellas not doing their job as they fly around, the cyclists pedalling through inches of rainwater – it's really quite scenic. On the cooler, wet days, the food we eat is comforting and nourishing, such as *Kitchuri* (page 138). When the weather is humid, we are more likely to eat cooling dishes such as *Shaak* (page 113). The wet season naturally affects the crops, so thrifty dishes of *Labra* (page 140) and *Chorchuri* (page 53), or even *Bhaja* (page 52) make their way onto our tables, to use up the vegetables before they rot. And wonderful *Maacher Pathuri* (page 147) made with the abundant river fish is another seasonal highlight.

As a city that has long welcomed people from neighbouring towns, cities and countries, many different communities have settled here over the years, and all have influenced the Kolkatan food scene, bringing their own ideas and creating new fusion cuisines that have played a big role in the food culture.

The city was a significant stop on the trading routes and also on the path to the hill stations, including tea estates like Darjeeling, so it absorbed new tastes and influences readily. The Chinese community that settled here created a fusion Indo-Chinese cuisine that became famous – and Kolkata's Chinatown is well worth a visit to sample it. Nahoum and Sons is a famous Jewish bakery in New Market that still sells exquisite cakes and pastries. The Nepalese community introduced their beloved *momos* to the street-food scene and they have become an essential part of the Kolkatan menu, widely available and much-loved. Mughlai (Indo-Persian) dishes, particularly kebabs and *biryani*, have found a comfortable place in home cooking and also in finer dining restaurants.

There are popular places to eat at any time of the day all over the city, from Deckers (Dacres) Lane, an extremely popular street in central Kolkata, with many small establishments serving up delicious lunchtime specials for the office workers in the area, to the fruit juice stalls in the New Market area, making the freshest *masombi* (a variety of orange) juice, year-round. Some of my other favourites include Nizam's, the birthplace of *kati rolls*, a street food unique to Kolkata; Arsalan for the Kolkatan *biryani*; and Mithai, for their traditional Benagli *sondesh*. These are just a few of the famous foodie spots you can visit.

Like most cities, there are definitely some must-see places in Kolkata: the Victoria Memorial being one, and the many temples, such as Kalighat, but also you must not fail to visit the fish and veg markets, the tea houses, including the Indian Coffee House in College Square, which is the oldest café in the city, and the many *saree* and little bangle shops that fill the streets. When you visit Kolkata, the hustle and bustle and aromas surround you and create a truly unique feeling that has to be experienced. In these pages, I have tried to give you a taste of this feeling and some ideas on what not to miss should you be lucky enough to visit this intoxicating city.

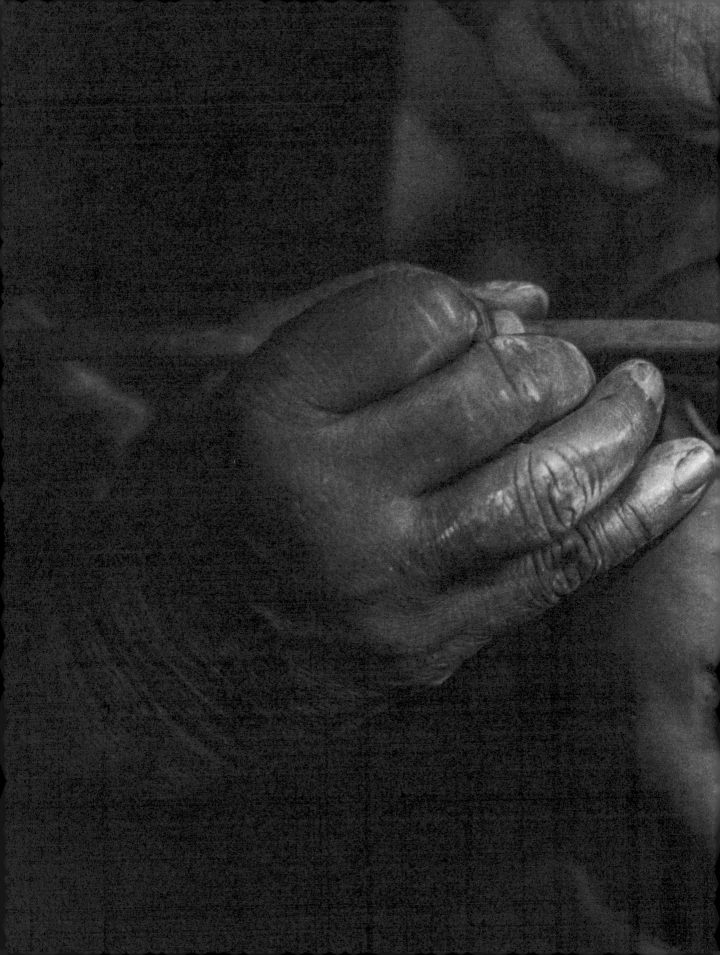

Before I take you into the nooks and crannies of the Bengali *rannaghar* (kitchen), there is something else you should know about how we serve dishes. Unlike many cuisines where a meal may be comprised of one or a few courses, in Bengali cuisine, all (and often that means many) dishes are served together, but they are eaten in specific combinations, one after the other. A classic order (and one that we use at our family table when entertaining and when in Kolkata) starts the meal with rice, followed by a bitter (*shukto* or *shaak*) palette cleanser, then a *dal* (a lentil dish) with a *bhaja* (battered fried vegetables), then a vegetable dish, a fish dish and next a meat dish, with a chutney and salad on the side. The dishes are eaten in that order and a little bit of rice is taken with each. A full Bengali meal can go on for hours and hours of preparation, and love and patience, is put into each dish. These days, if there is a special occasion or guests have been invited, this type of meal is laid out, otherwise in most Bengali households an everyday meal consists of rice, *dal*, a vegetable and either a meat or fish dish.

Food to me is not just a necessity – it is a powerful medium, a catalyst that connects history, hearts and emotions. It strengthens bonds and paves a long path of togetherness through nostalgia. When I decided to write this book, I realised at the same time that good food was the next most comforting thing I could think of after my loved ones. In the pages of this book I want to share some of the things I have experienced in Kolkata and learned from my family, my friends and my heritage, with the hope of touching hearts and lives in whatever small way I can.

So, let's tie on our aprons and decide what to create, shall we?

BREAKFAST

Breakfast is something Bengalis look forward to. Not just a meal to start the day, it is a meal of indulgence, a meal to relish, especially on the weekend, and particularly Sunday mornings. What we traditionally serve might surprise the western palate. Rich *luchi* (fried breads) and *shada aloor torkari* (potato curry) might sound like a recipe for indigestion at breakfast time, yet they are cooked week in, week out in many households. Eating such lavish, calorific and flavourful food in the morning is all about boosting the body's energy for the day ahead and also increasing our happy endorphins – heart or gut health is rarely considered in this respect! Many Bengalis have attempted over the years to adopt influences from other cultures for lighter, healthier breakfast meals on weekdays (such as boiled eggs or cereals), but weekends are all about going that extra mile and cooking the traditional dishes you will find in this chapter.

In Kolkata, breakfasts come in so many different varieties: street vendors serving tea and masala omelettes early in the morning; South Indian dishes such as *dosa* (rice and lentil pancakes) and *idli* (rice cakes) are also popular; and Zakaria Street is famous for its *tandoori roti* and *nihari* (a slow-cooked meat stew) – you will see people queuing from very early in the morning to get their orders in. The timeworn Maharaj restaurant in the Lake Market area is famous for their breakfasts of *radhaballabhi* (lentil-stuffed puris) and *torkari* (vegetable curries), served with *chai* (tea). They are a must-visit on any trip to the city.

On early weekend mornings, my family (and I'm sure many others) would relish spending time together talking about what would be cooked for breakfast and enjoying conversations about what successful bargaining had been done at the veg and fish markets. We would then sit down to a freshly cooked breakfast and, of course, the discussion around the table would focus on the rest of the meals that were going to be cooked that day! To work off the rich food, weekend mornings were for walks, or attending local community exercise groups, or yoga and meditation classes. I love Kolkata's famous Laughing Clubs, particuarly the one in the Lake Garden. These clubs are outdoor yoga sessions for young and old, where the excercises are designed to promote enjoyment and laughter – they are a wonderful sight and a beautiful way to start the day, with the smell of incense and the sounds of chanting mantras, ringing bells and laughter!

Bengali-Style French Toast

DIM PAURUTI

serves
2

Ask most college students or office-goers and they will all have their own favourite *kakur dokaner dim pauruti* (uncle's shop egg and bread). This is a popular morning street food that people from all walks of life eat, be they taxi or delivery drivers about to start their shifts, students, office workers or tourists. There are many variations of the history of this dish, but as it is very similar to French toast, many say it dates to colonial times. Traditionally, milk bread is used, which has a sweet taste similar to brioche. I have fond memories of eating *dim pauruti* on shiny silver paper plates at a café on Camac Street, just as the *saree* shops were opening, surrounded by all the office workers quickly eating up to get to work on time.

4 thick slices of brioche loaf

4 eggs

½ red onion, finely chopped

1 handful of finely chopped coriander (cilantro) (use the stalks too – they are full of flavour)

1 chilli, finely chopped

3 mm (⅛ in) piece of fresh ginger, grated (about ¼ teaspoon)

2 tablespoons milk

1 teaspoon salt

1 tablespoon butter

1 tablespoon rapeseed (canola) oil

ketchup, to serve

Toast the brioche slices to lightly brown each side and set aside.

Crack the eggs into a bowl and whisk, then add all of the other ingredients except the butter and oil.

Heat the butter and oil in a medium–large frying pan (skillet) (large enough to fit all the brioche slices in a single layer, although you can cook them individually if you wish) over a medium heat for about 1 minute, then gently pour the egg mixture into the pan. Cook for 1 minute, then place the brioche toasts on top of the egg mixture in each quarter of the pan, making sure they don't overlap.

Reduce the heat to medium–low and leave to cook for a further 4 minutes until the mixture has fully cooked through.

With a wooden spatula, cut the brioche omelette into quarters between each toast, if needed.

Serve two toasts on each plate with the cooked egg side facing upwards. Squeeze a bit of ketchup onto the side of the plate and enjoy!

Spiced Scrambled Eggs

DIMER BHURJI

serves
2

Although this is a dish traditionally made in Mumbai, as the trend for cafés in Kolkata has increased over the years, and breakfast options have widened, *dimer bhurji* has become very popular in the city. It's quick and easy to cook, and makes a filling start to the day. It is delicious with buttered toast and *Elaichi Cha* (page 160).

3 large eggs

¼ red onion, finely chopped

½ garlic clove, finely grated

½ tomato, finely chopped

2 handfuls of coriander (cilantro), finely chopped (use the stalks too)

½ chilli, finely chopped

1 spring onion (scallion), finely sliced

½ teaspoon chaat masala (readily available in Asian grocers or the spice aisle in supermarkets)

½ teaspoon salt

2 tablespoons milk

1 tablespoon butter, softened

1 tablespoon rapeseed (canola) oil, to cook

Crack the eggs into a medium mixing bowl and whisk well, then add all the other ingredients except the oil. Whisk again, ensuring everything is well combined.

Heat a medium frying pan (skillet) over a medium heat. Add the oil and heat for 1 minute, then carefully pour the egg mixture into the pan. Cook to scramble the eggs to your desired consistency.

Remove from the heat and serve immediately with buttered toast and a hot cup of tea.

Bengal Gram Dal

CHOLAR DAAL

serves
4

Earthy, nutty-tasting, slightly sweet and mellow, this dal is made with Bengal gram/channa dal. It is a classic Bengali dal, loved in every household, and a favourite Sunday family breakfast paired with *Luchi* (page 192). We use coconut and whole spices to elevate it. The dish is particularly made during religious festivals, as it does not contain onions and garlic – two *tamasic* foods (see page 142) that are avoided during *pujas*. Like many of the dishes in this book, every family has their own variation of *cholar daal* – this is ours.

150 g (generous ¾ cup) Bengal gram lentils (channa dal)

2 bay leaves

2.5 cm (1 in) piece of fresh ginger, finely grated

½ teaspoon ground turmeric

2 chillies, each halved lengthways

½ teaspoon ground cumin

½ teaspoon asafoetida

1½ teaspoons salt

1 teaspoon sugar

2 tablespoons mustard oil or rapeseed (canola) oil

10g (a small handful) thin dried coconut slices

1 cinnamon stick

3 green cardamom pods

4 cloves

1 teaspoon cumin seeds

½ x 400 g (14 oz) tin of organic coconut milk (use one with a high coconut content, above 75%)

½ teaspoon Jeera Bhaja Masala (see page 218)

2 teaspoons ghee

Luchi (see page 192), to serve

For best results, wash the lentils twice under cold running water, until the water is close to translucent, then leave to soak overnight or for a minimum of 2 hours. This speeds up the cooking process.

Once soaked and ready to cook, strain the lentils and place in a heavy-based medium saucepan with a lid. Add enough fresh water to cover the lentils by about 2.5cm (1 in). Place over a medium heat and bring to the boil. A white layer of foam will start to form while the dal is bubbling – carefully skim this off and discard. Simmer for 10–15 minutes.

Add a bay leaf, half of the grated ginger, the turmeric and 2 of the chilli halves, stir well and bring back to the boil, then reduce the heat to low and cook for 10–15 minutes until the lentils are soft but not broken, creamy and thick.

Add the ground cumin, asafoetida, salt and sugar, stir well and keep on a gentle simmer.

Meanwhile, heat 1 tablespoon of the oil in a small frying pan. Add the coconut slices and gently fry for about 1 minute on each side until lightly browned. Remove with tongs to drain on kitchen paper.

Add the remaining oil to the same pan and heat for 1 minute, then add the remaining bay leaf, cinnamon stick, cardamom pods, cloves and cumin seeds. Allow the spices to sizzle and release their aromas, taking care not to burn them. After 1 minute, add the remaining grated ginger and chilli halves, and stir well, taking care not to burn them.

Meanwhile, add the coconut milk to the dal pan and stir through, increasing the heat to medium.

Carefully pour the whole spices in oil into the pot of dal, then remove from the heat and immediately add the bhaja moshla and ghee. Stir well.

Transfer the dal to a serving dish and garnish with the fried coconut slices. Serve with freshly made *luchi*.

Pounded Rice with Vegetables

CHIRER PILAU

West Bengal is famous for its paddy fields and rice cultivation. Rice is a staple in Kolkata and there are so many different varieties. Basmati rice is most commonly known, but we tend to use different kinds for different dishes. In this recipe we use *chirey* or *chira*, which is parboiled rice that has been pounded flat and dried – you may find this sold as 'rice flakes' or under any of the following names: *chir, chirey, poha, powa* or *pawa*. It's used in many snack dishes, but this breakfast dish is one of my favourites, as it's so vibrant to look at and can have a variety of vegetables added to it – a perfect way to use up vegetables in the fridge.

1 potato, peeled and cut into 1 cm (½ in) cubes

1 carrot, peeled and cut into 1 cm (½ in) cubes

1 handful of green beans, topped and tailed and cut into 1 cm (½ in) pieces

125–150 g (4–5 oz) cauliflower, cut into the tiniest florets

100 g (3½ oz) frozen peas

250 g (2 generous cups) pounded rice (use the medium/thick type only)

2 tablespoons rapeseed (canola) oil

1½ teaspoons black mustard seeds

1 white onion, finely chopped

1 cm (½ in) piece of fresh ginger, grated

1 teaspoon sugar

1 green bird's eye chilli (or regular chilli to tone down the heat), slit lengthways

½ teaspoon ground turmeric

1 tablespoon whole redskin peanuts

1 tablespoon raisins

1 tablespoon chopped coriander (cilantro), including stalks

2 tablespoons freshly squeezed lemon juice

salt

Blanch the potatoes in a pan of boiling salted water for 3 minutes, then remove with a slotted spoon and set aside in a bowl.

Repeat the above step with the rest of the chopped vegetables, including the frozen peas, then drain and set aside in a separate bowl.

Place the pounded rice in a colander and wash it carefully, running it under gently flowing cold water for about 30 seconds. Leave to drain.

In the same pan used for blanching, heat 1 tablespoon of the oil over a medium heat. When hot, gently add the parboiled potatoes and cook for 4 minutes, allowing all sides to lightly brown. Remove the potatoes and return them to the bowl.

Add the remaining oil to the pan, then add the mustard seeds. When they start to crackle, add the onion and ginger. Stir well so they don't stick to the pan. Add the sugar and chilli, and cook until the onions become translucent. Add the potatoes, blanched vegetables, turmeric and 1½ teaspoons of salt, and mix well. Carefully add the drained pounded rice, peanuts, raisins and coriander, and mix very gently so that the pounded rice doesn't break up. Cook for a further 4 minutes, then remove from the heat.

Drizzle the lemon juice over just before serving and enjoy.

White Potato Curry

SHADA ALOOR TORKARI

serves 4

One of the simplest yet tastiest *torkaris* on the Bengali menu, sometimes called *aloo chechki*, this pairs perfectly with *luchi* (puffed fried breads, page 192) and is a beautifully flavourful dish. I first tasted it at my friend Debarun's place one Sunday morning. Made lovingly by his mother, it had the perfect balance of sweet, salt and spice heat. This highlights one of the differences between the cooking styles of East and West Bengal. Kolkata's indigenous people are the *Ghoti* but there is also a large population of *Bangals* from East Bengal who moved to the west after partition in 1947. Traditionally, *Ghotis* use more sugar in their cooking, hence its inclusion here. Every household has a different version of this curry and my family recipe is completely no-fuss! This *torkari* uses minimal spices and isn't very rich, making it a perfect breakfast dish.

1½ tablespoons mustard oil or vegetable oil

1 teaspoon nigella seeds

2 bird's eye chillies, slit in half lengthways

4 potatoes, washed, peeled and cut into 1.5 cm (¾ in) cubes

¼ teaspoon sugar

1 teaspoon salt

½ teaspoon asafoetida (optional)

125 ml (½ cup) water

1 tablespoon chopped coriander (cilantro), to garnish

Luchi (see page 192), to serve

Place a heavy-based pan that has a lid over a medium heat and add the mustard or vegetable oil. Allow to heat for 1 minute, then add the nigella seeds and chillies. These should start to sizzle as soon as they are placed in the oil. Add the cubed potatoes to the hot temper and cook for 4–5 minutes, stirring constantly so the potatoes don't stick to the bottom of the pan. Add the sugar, salt and asafoetida, and stir well to ensure the potatoes have been fully coated. Cook for a further 6 minutes, then add the water, stir well and bring to the boil.

Reduce the heat to low, cover with a lid and cook for 15 minutes until the potatoes are cooked through. If they are taking slightly longer to cook, ensure there is enough water in the pan, and allow to simmer until the potatoes are soft, just starting to break apart and coated with a thick gravy.

Garnish with chopped coriander and serve with hot *luchi* on the side.

Yellow Pea Curry

GHUGNI

serves
4

Whether this dish is enjoyed on a Kolkata street, served on a small steel plate garnished with red onions and chillies, or in the comfort of a Bengali household as a Sunday breakfast with *luchi* (see page 192), it's a classic! It's not just a breakfast dish either. Back in London, my memories of *ghugni* are of a Sunday afternoon snack eaten at the kitchen table, talking, laughing and waiting for the family dinner to be cooked. Every so often my parents would make this as a starter for guests, and they would add very small cubes of lamb in too, to add to the depth of flavour. As a cheat, or if you're pressed for time, you can use tinned chickpeas (garbanzo beans) for this recipe, but for the authentic *ghugni* texture we use whole yellow peas, also known as motor dal.

250 g (scant 1½ cups) whole yellow peas (motor dal)

2 bay leaves

6 cloves

1 cinnamon stick

3.5 cm (1½ in) piece of fresh ginger: 2.5 cm (1 in) cut into long fine strips; 1 cm (½ in) grated

1½ teaspoons ground turmeric

1½ tablespoons mustard oil or rapeseed (canola) oil

2 green cardamom pods, lightly crushed

1 teaspoon cumin seeds

2 dried red chillies

1 onion, finely chopped

1½ teaspoons sugar

2 garlic cloves, grated

1 potato, cut into 1 cm (½ in) cubes

2 tomatoes, diced

1½ teaspoons ground cumin

1½ teaspoons ground coriander

1 teaspoon tamarind paste diluted with 2 tablespoons water

1 teaspoon salt, or to taste

To finish

1 teaspoon Barir Bhaja Masala (page 218)

1 tablespoon finely chopped coriander (cilantro)

lime wedges

In a large bowl, wash the yellow peas a couple of times under fresh running water, then place in a bowl, cover with 5 cm (2 in) water and leave to soak for at least 12 hours or overnight.

Drain, then carefully transfer the peas to a large, heavy-based pan using a teacup as a measure. Use the same cup to top up the pan with double the amount of water. Place over a medium heat and bring to a simmer. A thin, white layer of foam will appear – gently skim off and discard. Add 1 bay leaf, 3 cloves, the cinnamon stick, all the ginger strips and ½ teaspoon of the turmeric. Simmer for a further 20 minutes over a medium–low heat until the peas are semi-soft when squeezed but are still whole.

Drain the peas (along with the whole spices) in a colander set over a bowl. Set the peas and cooking water aside.

Place the same pan back over a medium heat and add the oil. When hot, add the remaining bay leaf and cloves along with the cardamom pods. After 30 seconds, add the cumin seeds and the dried chillies. Cook until the aromas release, taking care not to burn the spices. Add the onions and cook, stirring, until translucent. Mix in ½ teaspoon of the sugar, then after 1 minute add the grated garlic and ginger. Cook for

1 minute, then add the potatoes and cook for 3 minutes, stirring regularly. When the potatoes start to take on a little colour, add the tomatoes and 1 teaspoon of salt. Mix well and cook for a further 4–5 minutes, stirring.

When the tomatoes have broken down, add the remaining 1 teaspoon of turmeric along with the ground cumin and coriander. Mix well and cook for about 2 minutes, then add the yellow peas. Stir to ensure the peas are well coated in the spices. Cook for a further 4 minutes over a low heat.

Add 500 ml (2 cups) of the reserved cooking water and increase the heat to medium. Bring to the boil, then reduce the heat to low, cover and simmer for a further 15–20 minutes until the water has reduced. The desired consistency is a semi-thick gravy with whole but soft yellow peas.

Increase the heat to medium again, add the diluted tamarind paste and mix well. Add the remaining ½ teaspoon of sugar and more salt to taste, stir well and remove from the heat. Sprinkle over the barir bhaja moshla and the chopped coriander, and keep covered until ready to serve.

Serve in bowls with wedges of lime on the side. You can eat with *luchi,* too.

Rich Tomato and New Potato Curry

ALOOR DOM

serves 4

Aloor dom is a rich, thick-gravied dish made with new potatoes (*notun aloo*). The potatoes are soft but stay whole, immersed in intense flavours. This evokes childhood memories for me, of sitting on my grandmother's balcony, among her claypot flowers with the sun beating down, eating puffed *luchi* (page 192) and steaming *aloor dom* – sheer joy and contentment. It's a comfort food that creates a happy place for me whenever we make it at home. The aromas of the whole spices fill the kitchen, transporting me to my childhood summer holidays.

500 g (1 lb 2 oz) new potatoes

1½ teaspoons ground turmeric

2 tablespoons mustard oil or rapeseed (canola) oil

1½ teaspoons Paanch Phoron (page 218)

1 bay leaf

3 green cardamom pods

1 cinnamon stick

1 white onion, finely chopped

2 teaspoons sugar

1 cm (½ in) piece of fresh ginger, grated

2 tomatoes, roughly chopped

1 teaspoon ground cumin

1 teaspoon ground coriander

2 teaspoons tomato purée (paste)

2 whole dried red chillies

1 teaspoon Barir Bhaja Masala (page 218)

1 teaspoon ghee

salt, to taste

Luchi (see page 192), to serve

Wash the potatoes, leaving the skins on, and place them in a heavy-based medium saucepan. Cover with water and add a generous pinch of salt, then bring to the boil. Cook for 7 minutes, then drain and allow to cool.

Peel the cooled potatoes, then place in a mixing bowl, add the turmeric and toss well to ensure the potatoes are thoroughly coated.

Heat 1 tablespoon of the oil in the same pan, return the potatoes to the pan and cook for about 5 minutes until they begin to colour slightly and blister. Remove from the heat and return the potatoes to the mixing bowl.

Add the remaining oil to the pan over a medium heat. Add the paanch phoron, bay leaf, cardamom pods and cinnamon stick, and cook until their aromas release, making sure they don't burn. Add the onion and cook, stirring, for 1 minute, then add 1 teaspoon of the sugar. Cook until the onions are slightly translucent, then add the ginger and tomatoes, and cook for a further 2 minutes.

Meanwhile, combine the ground cumin and coriander with the tomato purée and the remaining 1 teaspoon of sugar in a bowl. Add 2 tablespoons of cold water and mix well to form a thick paste (this stops the powdered spices from burning). Add this mixture along with the whole dried chillies to the onion pan, stirring well, and cook for 2 minutes. Add 200 ml (scant 1 cup) water and stir well, then bring to a gentle boil. Add the turmeric potatoes and stir well, then add 1½ teaspoons of salt, or to taste. Cook over a medium heat for about 7 minutes, then reduce the heat, cover and simmer for a further 15–20 minutes, stirring halfway through.

When cooked, the potatoes should be soft in the middle but still whole and the gravy should be thick and rich. If the gravy is still too watery, increase the heat and allow the water to bubble away with the pan lid off. Sprinkle in the bhaja masala and add the ghee, gently stir through just once and remove from the heat. Serve with freshly made *luchi*.

For Bengalis, lunch is widely thought to be the most important meal of the day. India is a tropical country, hot and humid, and so by lunchtime fatigue often sets in. A rejuvenating lunch is instrumental in reviving people enough to go about the rest of their day.

On any given day, most households would be found making rice and a fish curry for lunch. A traditional Bengali lunch table is commonly set with rice, a dal, a vegetable and a fish dish. The type of dal is often determined by the season – I've given you a *Moong daal* recipe (page 49) using fine green beans, because I find that it can be made at any time of the year and adapted to the produce available. The vegetable dish might be a medley of mixed veg (*Shukto*, see page 69) or a single veg dry-fry, depending on what is on offer in the markets that morning or whatever is in the fridge.

Office workers will often take a tiffin carrier to work. Early morning Kolkatan households are a hive of activity as freshly prepared food is packaged up in these tiered stainless-steel carriers with 3–4 layers containing rice or breads, a dal, a vegetable *thorkari*, and a meat/fish dish. *Tiffinwallas* can also collect the container and deliver it by rickshaw to the client at work, allowing food to reach the consumer in an eco-friendly, neat and organised manner.

For those who don't have a packed lunch, the small street-food shacks around the city cater for every taste. Each one usually specialises in just a few dishes, and a meal will consist of a heap of rice surrounded by small servings of curries, often served in *shal patha* leaf bowls. For a few hours over lunch, the tempo in pockets of the city steps up a gear or two. In the famous Decker's (Dacres) Lane, a pedestrian-only thoroughfare in the Esplanade area, rows of benches are laid along the street and interspersed with a plethora of hole-in-the-wall eateries and street carts on wheels, all serving up a cacophony of tastes, aromas and sounds, creating a buzzing atmosphere. Office workers sit eating their lunches off stainless-steel trays perched on their laps. Once finished, a young man allocated to each shop knows which plate to collect to be washed ready for the next sitting of customers. Although at first it may seem like chaos, a synchronised harmony seems to emerge in those few hours of trading, allowing the throngs of people to efficiently finish lunch in good time and good spirits.

The recipes in this chapter can also be eaten as part of dinner, as there is no hard and fast rule dictating which dishes should be eaten when. I've chosen ones that I regularly prepared while living in Kolkata. *Dhoka'r dalna* (page 66) paired with *Moong daal* (page 49) and a tomato salad and served with rice makes a delicious wholesome vegan meal. The *Kumro'r chokka* (page 59) and *Dimer dalna* (page 46) eaten with breads make another great lunch combo, best topped with a raita to add a crunchy, sour note. Feel free to pair dishes from other chapters as you wish.

Eggs in a Rich Thick Gravy

DIMER DALNA

serves
4

An egg curry is a popular dish throughout India, but each region has their own way of cooking it. Eggs are cheap, easy to get hold of and an essential item on the shopping list for most households. This dish takes me back to the long train journeys we would make as a family. My gran would pack this delicious egg curry and some dry *rooti* in tiffin carriers. Often travelling with the extended family, we would sit on the different tiers of the carriage (adults at the bottom, kids in the middle and on top) eating these packed dinners on disposable plates. It is a rich, flavoursome curry with a dry, thick gravy and can be made from chicken or duck eggs.

4 large eggs, at room temperature

2 potatoes, peeled and quartered

1½ teaspoons ground turmeric

1 white onion, quartered

2 garlic cloves

2.5 cm (1 in) piece of fresh ginger, peeled and cut in half

2 tomatoes, roughly chopped

3 tablespoons mustard oil or rapeseed (canola) oil

1 bay leaf

1 cinnamon stick

2 green cardamom pods, lightly crushed

3 cloves

1 dried red chilli

1 teaspoon cumin seeds

1 teaspoon sugar

1 teaspoon ground cumin

1 teaspoon ground coriander

1 teaspoon Bengali Garam Masala (see page 218)

½ teaspoon dried fenugreek leaves

1 handful of chopped coriander (cilantro) leaves

salt, to taste

Place the eggs in a saucepan, cover with water and bring to the boil. Continue to cook at a rolling boil for a further 6 minutes. Drain and transfer the boiled eggs to a bowl of cold water to cool.

Refill the same saucepan with water and bring to the boil. Add a generous pinch of salt and the potatoes. Boil for 5 minutes, then drain and place in a separate bowl. Add ¼ teaspoon of the turmeric and ¼ teaspoon salt and mix with a spoon until the potatoes are well coated. Set aside.

When the eggs have cooled, peel and wash each egg to ensure no pieces of shell remain. Use a knife to very gently make 2–3 shallow diagonal slits in each egg, about 2.5 mm (⅛ in) deep and 2 cm (¾ in) long. Repeat this pattern around each egg, then place in a bowl. Add ¼ teaspoon of the turmeric and ¼ teaspoon of salt, then toss the eggs until they are all well coated. Set aside.

In a blender, blitz the onions, garlic, ginger and tomatoes, along with 2 tablespoons water, to a thick paste.

Heat 1½ tablespoons of the oil in a pan that has a lid over a medium heat. When hot, add the eggs and cook for about 3 minutes, turning them every 30 seconds. The eggs should lightly brown in places. Remove to a bowl with a slotted spoon.

Add the potatoes to the pan and cook for about 2 minutes on each side, allowing them to lightly brown on each side. Scoop them out and place them back in their bowl.

Add the remaining oil to the pan. When hot, add the bay leaf, cinnamon stick, cardamom pods, cloves, dried chilli and cumin seeds. Cook until the aromas are released, taking care not to burn the spices. Add the onion paste and stir – it will sizzle a bit, so take care. Cook for 3 minutes, then add 1 teaspoon of salt, the sugar, ground spices (including the remaining teaspoon of turmeric) and the fenugreek leaves. Mix to a thick paste, ensuring it is well combined.

Add 250 ml (1 cup) water and bring to the boil. Add the eggs and potatoes back to the pan and bring to a gentle simmer. Check the seasoning, then reduce the heat to low and cover with a lid. Cook for a further 6 minutes until the potatoes are fully cooked and the gravy is thick and rich. If there is still liquid in the pan, increase the heat, remove the lid and allow the gravy to reduce to your desired consistency.

Sprinkle with chopped coriander and cover again until you are ready to serve. This is lovely with *Rootis* (page 197) and *Barir* salad (page 208).

Dry-Roasted Moong Dal with Green Beans

BHAJA MOONG DAAL

serves
4

This is an earthy and comforting dal made with yellow split lentils. In this recipe, we dry-roast the lentils first to give them a nutty taste. In Kolkata, *moong daal* is often served at religious festivals as it is a *satvic* dish using no onions or garlic. In our family, we add fine green beans, to add an extra layer of texture (but you could also use peas or other veg, adapting it to use whatever seasonal produce is available). This dal is delicately tempered with minimal spices. Serve with white rice, another *bhaja* (*Aloo Bhaja*, page 52, or *Phulkopi Bhaja*, page 65) and a dash of lime (or if you are in Kolkata, I would recommend the *ghondoraaj lebu* lime). Here, I have made it in a heavy-based pot, but you can also cook this in a pressure cooker, which speeds up the process.

150 g (generous ¾ cup) yellow lentils (moong dal)

550 ml (2¼ cups) water

¾ teaspoon ground turmeric

50 g (2 oz) fine green beans, topped and tailed, washed and drained

1 teaspoon ghee

1½ teaspoons salt, or to taste

For the temper

1 tablespoon rapeseed (canola) oil

1 bay leaf

1½ teaspoons cumin seeds

2 cm (¾ in) piece of fresh ginger, grated

½ teaspoon asafoetida

Roast the lentils in a shallow, dry frying pan (skillet) over a medium heat for about 3 minutes, continuously tossing them until the aromas release and some of the lentils turn a light brown. Keep an eye on the pan, as they can burn very quickly.

Remove from the heat and transfer to a medium heavy-based pot. Gently run the lentils under cold water, washing until the water runs clear. Finally, fill the pot with the measured water, place back over a medium heat and bring to a simmer, skimming off the foam that rises to the surface. Stir in the turmeric, cover, reduce the heat and cook for a further 15 minutes until

the lentils are soft, but not totally broken down. Add the green beans and bring back to a simmer while you make the temper.

In a small saucepan, heat the oil over a medium heat, then add the bay leaf and cumin seeds. Cook for 1 minute, then add the ginger and asafoetida. Stir gently and cook for a further 2 minutes.

Pour all of the temper into the dal (it may crackle slightly) and stir well. Season with salt, to taste. Remove from the heat and add the ghee. Stir through once and cover until ready to serve.

Chicken Stew

CHICKEN ISHTEW

serves 4

Made famous during the time of the British Raj, the chicken *ishtew* is a light and simple Anglo-Indian dish made with fresh chicken, chunky vegetables and a wholesome gravy. The aromas of the whole spices are highlighted, especially the black peppercorns.

Chitto Babu'r Dokan is a small shop in Decker's (Dacres) Lane – a busy lane, bustling with food vendors who serve all the office workers – and is famous for its chicken *ishtew* and toast. During the lunchtime rush, you will find its lines of benches full of people and alive with noise and fantastic aromas.

1 tablespoon rapeseed (canola) oil

2 teaspoons unsalted butter

3 bay leaves

2 shallots, cut into quarters

2 cm (¾ in) piece of fresh ginger, grated

1 garlic clove, grated

1 teaspoon sugar

10 whole black peppercorns

5 cloves

500 g (1 lb 2 oz) bone-in skinless chicken thighs

2 potatoes, peeled and cut into quarters

2 carrots, peeled and cut into 4 cm (1½ in) batons

150 g (5 oz) green papaya, peeled and cut into 2 cm (¾ in) cubes (available in Indian grocery stores)

2 teaspoons Bengali Garam Masala (see page 218)

250 ml (1 cup) fresh chicken stock

250 ml (1 cup) full-fat milk

100 g (3½ oz) fine green beans, trimmed and halved

salt and freshly ground black pepper, to taste

Set a heavy-based pan over a medium heat and add the oil and butter. After 1 minute, add the bay leaves and shallots. Cook, stirring, until the shallots start to become translucent, then add the ginger and garlic. Cook until the raw smell diminishes, then add the sugar, peppercorns and cloves. Cook, stirring, for 1 minute, then add the chicken thighs and potatoes. Cook for 5 minutes, stirring.

Add the carrots, papaya and garam masala to the pan, mix well and cook for a further 8 minutes, stirring now and then to make sure nothing sticks to the bottom of the pan.

Add the chicken stock and milk, stir and bring to a gentle simmer. Check for salt and adjust to taste, then reduce to a low heat and cover the pan. Cook for 15–20 minutes, stirring in the green beans after 10 minutes and re-covering the pan until the time is up.

Check that the chicken is cooked through and that the potatoes and carrots are soft, then remove from the heat and keep covered until ready to serve.

To serve, pour into a bowl and grind over some fresh black pepper. Serve with warm buttered toast.

Fried Potatoes

ALOO BHAJA

serves
4

These are fine strips of potato, fried and enjoyed freshly cooked. Served with boiled rice, *Masoor Dal* (page 110) and a wedge of *gondhoraj lebu* lime, it makes a simple yet fulfilling meal. Often, people will have this as one course and then move on to the meat and fish dishes afterwards, but it can also be a meal in itself. The dash of lime elevates the dish – although we can't get the *gondhoraj lebu* variety outside India, substituting it for a regular lime does the job just as well.

3 white potatoes, peeled and washed

½ teaspoon ground turmeric

½ teaspoon salt

mustard/rapeseed (canola) oil, for shallow frying

To serve

Masoor Dal (page 110)

boiled rice

lime wedges, for squeezing

Cut the potatoes into discs about 5 mm (¼ in) thick. Place the discs on top of each other and cut lengthways again into slices about 5 mm (¼ in) thick. This should give you long strips of potatoes that are not too thin.

Place all the potato strips in a bowl and add the turmeric and salt. Mix well, ensuring each potato strip is coated with the seasoning. Leave to rest for 5–7 minutes.

Meanwhile, heat a 2 cm (¾ in) depth of oil in a frying pan (skillet) over a medium–high heat.

Take a handful of the marinaded potato strips at a time and slowly release into the oil. Take care as it may splatter. Cook for 4–5 minutes, turning halfway through. The potatoes will begin to turn a light brown colour – at this point, take one potato strip out and check whether it's cooked through. If so, remove the potatoes with a slotted spoon and place on a plate lined with kitchen paper to drain.

Repeat with the remaining potato.

Serve with hot *masoor dal*, steaming rice and a dash of lime juice.

Semi-Dry Seasonal Vegetable Medley

CHORCHURI

serves
4

This is one of those dishes that is perfect for using up vegetables in the fridge. I feel it also encourages the no-waste policy, as you can use stalks, ends and all the bits of vegetables that usually you'd have to think twice about. It's cooked with the Bengali five spice and turmeric, so it really allows the flavours of the seasonal vegetables to come through and be celebrated.

The winter months see the most variety of fresh vegetables in Kolkata, and they are just so plump and tasty. One particular market we used to go to in Gariahut sold such a wide variety that it was a treat to see – I loved the different shades of green and the unique way the stallholders displayed their vegetables to attract the customer. Each vendor, or *shobjiwala*, would sit surrounded by their products and often they might specialise in only one type of veg, but the display would always be impressive.

For this recipe, I've used vegetables that you should find readily available, but feel free to experiment and use other vegetables too.

---

3 tablespoons mustard oil or rapeseed (canola) oil

2 teaspoons Paanch Phoron (page 218)

1 green bird's eye chilli, slit lengthways

1 potato, washed well, cut into 1 cm (½ in) cubes with skin on

100 g (3½ oz) pumpkin, peeled and cut into 1.5 cm (⅔ in) cubes

100 g (3½ oz) cauliflower, cut into very small florets (the stalk can be used too, cut into 1 cm/½ in cubes)

80 g (3 oz) eggplant (aubergine), cut into 1.5 cm (⅔ in) cubes

80 g (3 oz) okra (ladies' fingers), cut into 1 cm (½ in) rings

80 g (3 oz) fine green beans, cut into 1 cm (½ in) pieces

½ teaspoon sugar

1 teaspoon ground turmeric

1 teaspoon salt, or to taste

Place a wok or karai over a medium heat and add 2 tablespoons of the oil. When hot, add the paanch phoron and cook until the aromas are released, then carefully add the chilli. Let it sizzle for 30 seconds, then add the potatoes. Cook, stirring, for about 4 minutes, then add the pumpkin and cauliflower. Mix well and cook for a further 4–5 minutes until the vegetables begin to brown slightly. Take care not to let them brown too much.

Add the remaining vegetables, sugar and turmeric, mix well and sauté for about 5 minutes. Stir through 1 teaspoon of salt, then reduce the heat and cover the pan with a lid. Cook for a further 10 minutes.

Remove the lid and make sure the potatoes are fully cooked. The *chorchuri* should have a slightly mashed up texture and be semi-dry. When the vegetables are cooked through, check the seasoning and add more salt if desired. Drizzle the remaining tablespoon of oil on top of the *chorchuri*, then cover until ready to serve.

Bottle Gourd with Shrimp

LAU CHINGRI

serves
4

This is typically a summer dish, as the *lau* 'bottle gourd' (or calabash) is grown during the summer months. Light green in colour, this squash-like vegetable contains a lot of water, which has cooling properties for the body. It is easy to digest too. During cooking, the water is absorbed and it is served as a dry-fry dish.

Most households have their own recipe for this and the one below is from the lady who used to cook for me during my stay in Kolkata. In India, having home-help is quite common and my cook lady found it very funny when I would ask to watch her cook or even assist her, so that I could learn.

350 g (12 oz) small cooked shrimp (prawns), peeled

1 teaspoon ground turmeric

1 teaspoon salt

500–600 g (1 lb 2 oz–1 lb 5 oz) bottle gourd (calabash)

2 tablespoons mustard oil or rapeseed (canola) oil

1½ teaspoons cumin seeds

1 green bird's eye chilli, cut in half lengthways

1 cm (½ in) piece of fresh ginger, grated

1 teaspoon sugar

1 teaspoon ghee

½ teaspoon Bhaja Jeera Masala (see page 218)

steamed rice, to serve

In a small bowl, combine the shrimp with ½ teaspoon each of the ground turmeric and salt, and mix well. Leave to marinate for at least 10 minutes.

Meanwhile, peel the bottle gourd and cut into 5 mm (¼ in) discs. Look out for the large seeds – if any are present, discard them. Stacking a couple of discs at a time, cut the discs into long strips, each about 5 mm (¼ in) thick.

Heat the oil in a karai or wok over a medium heat, then add the cumin seeds and the green chilli. Cook until the aromas release, then add the grated ginger. Stir for 1 minute,

ensuring the ginger doesn't stick to the base of the pan, then add the bottle gourd strips and cook for 4 minutes, stirring all the time. Add the shrimp and stir well. Cook for 3 minutes, then add the remaining salt, turmeric and the sugar. Mix well and cook for a further 10 minutes until most of the water has evaporated.

Add the ghee and give everything a final mix, then remove from the heat and sprinkle the bhaja jeera masala around the dish. Cover until ready to serve.

Serve with steamed rice.

Sweet Pumpkin with Black Chickpeas

KUMRO'R CHOKKA

serves 4

Using fresh seasonal vegetables in Kolkata is part of daily life, and going to the vegetable markets early in the morning is an everyday activity in most households. The winter months are best as the choice of vegetables is just so vast. The rows and rows of veg sellers shout out the day's bargains or specials to catch your attention, and the produce is still measured out by hand on scales. The displays that some of the stallholders create is a treat for the eyes, with all the colours in every shade. It's a lovely experience.

This is a very common winter dish. The sweetness of the pumpkin with the heat from the spices and the creaminess of the black chickpeas (Bengal gram) makes this a perfect dish to serve with *luchis* (puffed fried breads, page 192).

---

2 tablespoons mustard oil or rapeseed (canola) oil

2 bay leaves

1 whole dried red chilli

1 teaspoon Paanch Phoron (page 218)

2 creamy potatoes, peeled and cut into 1.5 cm (⅔ in) cubes

500 g (1 lb 2 oz) pumpkin, peeled and cut into 2 cm (¾ in) cubes (peeled weight)

1 teaspoon ground turmeric

1 teaspoon ground cumin

½ teaspoon chilli powder

1 teaspoon Bengali Garam Masala (page 218)

2 teaspoons asafoetida

2.5 cm (1 in) piece of fresh ginger, grated

2 tablespoons Greek-style yoghurt

1½ teaspoon salt

1 teaspoon sugar

1 x 400 g (14 oz) tin of kala chana (black chickpeas/Bengal gram), drained

1 teaspoon Barir Bhaja Masala (see page 218)

1 teaspoon chopped coriander (cilantro), to garnish

Heat a heavy-based pan that has a lid over a medium heat and add the oil. When hot, add the bay leaves and dried chilli, allowing them to crackle slightly for about 30 seconds, then add the paanch phoron and cook for another 30 seconds. Add the potatoes and fry for about 5 minutes, stirring frequently to ensure that they don't stick to the bottom of the pan. Mix in the pumpkin.

Meanwhile, combine the turmeric, cumin, chilli powder, garam masala, asafoetida, ginger and yoghurt in a small bowl. Add 1 tablespoon of water and mix together.

Add the spice mixture to the pan and stir well, ensuring all the vegetable cubes are well coated. Cook for a further 8 minutes.

The *chokka* is now starting to take shape. Add 125 ml (½ cup) water, then add the salt and sugar. Mix well and bring back to a simmer for 5 minutes. Add the kala chana and mix well, then bring back to a simmer. Cover the pan, reduce the heat to low and cook for a further 15 minutes, or until the potatoes are soft. By now, the water should have been absorbed into the potatoes and pumpkin leaving a thick coating on the veg, which may also be slightly broken and mushy. This is the perfect consistency.

Finally, add the bhaja masala and give one final stir. Remove from the heat and keep covered until ready to serve.

Just before serving, sprinkle with coriander.

Smoky Chargrilled Eggplant

BEGUN PORA

serves 4

Some say this is the Bengali version of *baba ganoush*. The dish is smoky and little spicy, and also pungent and crunchy with the onions. Many regions in India have their own version, and they can involve quite a few ingredients, but this one is simple and allows the eggplant to be the star of the show.

Surprisingly, I never liked this dish when I was growing up, but now it's a dish we make quite regularly as a family, especially in the summer when we can put the eggplant on the barbecue to chargrill.

2 eggplant (aubergines)
1 tablespoon mustard oil
½ white onion, finely chopped
5 mm (¼ in) piece of fresh ginger, very thinly sliced into strips
1 handful of chopped coriander (cilantro)
1 green bird's eye chilli, finely chopped
1 teaspoon salt, or to taste

To serve

Rooti (page 197)

sliced onions

Wash the eggplant and dry them with kitchen paper. Score 5 slits, about 5 mm (¼ in) deep, into each eggplant lengthways. Brush each with a little of the oil.

If you have a gas hob, very carefully place each eggplant directly on the flame of a burner and cook, turning regularly with tongs, until the skin becomes charred all over. If you don't have a gas hob, this can be done over a barbecue. Remove from the heat and place in a bowl. Cover the bowl with a lid and leave to cool.

When the eggplant are cool enough to be handled, carefully pull away the skins and discard. Take care not to take too much of the flesh off with the skin. Place the eggplant flesh on a chopping board and roughly chop into very small pieces – you want it to be rather mushy. Transfer to a bowl, then add the remaining ingredients and mix well, adding salt to taste.

Serve at room temperature with *rooti* and sliced onions.

Cauliflower Dry-Fry

PHULKOPI BHAJA

serves
4

A winter classic in Kolkata. Cauliflowers have a special place in Bengalis' hearts and stomachs! This vegetable is so versatile that it's added to many vegetable dishes and also fish dishes. The recipe is an uncomplicated one with minimal ingredients, allowing the flavour of the cauliflower to take the limelight.

This is a childhood favourite in our household, especially on the weekends when my mother would serve it with puffed *luchi* (fried breads, page 192) and plain yoghurt on the side.

1 tablespoon mustard oil or rapeseed (canola) oil

1 teaspoon nigella seeds

1 whole dried red chilli

250 g (9 oz) cauliflower, washed and broken into very small florets

½ teaspoon ground turmeric

1 teaspoon salt, or to taste

1 handful of finely chopped coriander (cilantro) leaves

Place a shallow frying pan (skillet) over a medium heat, add the oil and heat for 1 minute. Add the nigella seeds and dried chilli and stir for 1 minute, taking care not to burn the whole spices. Add the cauliflower, mix well and cook for 3–4 minutes before adding the turmeric and salt to taste. Sir well and cook for a further 3 minutes.

Reduce the heat and cover the pan with a lid. Cook for a further 5 minutes until the cauliflower is soft and cooked through and any water it has released has evaporated, removing the lid and increasing the heat after 5 minutes, if needed, to bubble away any remaining liquid.

Sprinkle with coriander and cover until ready to serve.

Place on a serving dish and serve with hot *Rooti* (page 197) or *Luchi* and some *Begun achar* (eggplant pickle, page 216) as a light lunch.

Lentil Cakes in Gravy

DHOKA'R DALNA

serves 4

For the lentil cakes

250 g (1½ cups) Bengal gram lentils (channa dal), soaked in water overnight

1 tablespoon desiccated (dried unsweetened shredded) coconut

2 cm (¾ in) piece of fresh ginger, grated

1 green chilli, roughly chopped

1 teaspoon asafoetida

½ teaspoon carom seeds

1 teaspoon ground cumin

1 teaspoon sugar

1 teaspoon salt

1 tablespoon rapeseed (canola) oil

1 teaspoon cumin seeds

vegetable oil, for greasing and shallow-frying

2 tablespoons plain (all-purpose) flour

For the gravy

2 tablespoons mustard oil

2 potatoes, peeled and quartered

1½ teaspoons cumin seeds

1 bay leaf

1 cinnamon stick

4 green cardamom pods, lightly crushed

2.5 cm (1 in) piece of fresh ginger, grated

2 tomatoes, roughly chopped

1 teaspoon ground cumin

½ teaspoon ground coriander

1 teaspoon Bengali Garam Masala (see page 218)

1 teaspoon ground turmeric

1 teaspoon sugar

1 green bird's eye chilli, slit lengthways

1 teaspoon salt, or to taste

1 teaspoon ghee

This has to be one of my favourite vegetarian dishes of all time. It is a *Satvic* recipe (no garlic or onions are used in it), so is a popular dish for religious festivities. It does require patience to make it, as it's a long process with two stages of cooking, but the results are so worth it. This dish was usually made when my parents had invited guests for dinner and we would look forward to the leftovers the next day, when the lentil cakes had absorbed more of the gravy.

Start with the lentil cakes. Drain the soaked lentils and put them in a blender along with the coconut, ginger, chilli, asafoetida, carom seeds, ground cumin, sugar and salt. Add about 5 tablespoons of water and blend to a semi-coarse mixture. Do not make the paste too smooth or the lentil cakes will break when frying.

Heat a karai or wok over a medium heat and add the tablespoon of rapeseed oil. When hot, add the cumin seeds and cook until the aromas release. Carefully add the spice paste – it will sizzle. Cook for 6 minutes, stirring constantly to ensure the mixture doesn't stick to the bottom of the pan. The mixture will begin to thicken as the water evaporates. Continue to stir until the mixture starts to look like a dough, then remove from the heat.

Oil the work surface with 1 tablespoon of vegetable oil. Place the lentil mixture on the surface and use a straight-edged spatula to flatten it out into a square shape, about 2 cm (¾ in) thick. Smooth out the edges and top. Carefully divide the square into 20 equal small squares and gently separate each one on the work surface.

Heat enough oil for shallow-frying in a karai, wok or deep frying pan (skillet).

Meanwhile, put the flour in a small bowl and add 6 tablespoons of water. Mix to a thin white paste.

When the oil is hot, take a lentil square and dip it in the flour paste. Ensure is is well coated, then gently lower it into the hot oil. Repeat with all the lentil squares, ensuring you don't add too many in one go. Fry for about 4 minutes until the lentil cakes begin to turn a golden colour. Remove from the oil with a slotted spoon and place on a plate lined with kitchen paper to drain.

Repeat until all the lentil cakes are cooked and set them aside.

Method continues overleaf

Next, make the gravy. Place a separate karai or wok that has a lid over a medium heat and add the mustard oil. Once hot, add the potatoes and cook for 6 minutes, stirring occasionally until lightly browned. Remove with a slotted spoon to a plate and set aside.

To the same pan, add the cumin seeds, bay leaf, cinnamon stick and cardamom pods. Cook until the aromas release, then stir in the ginger and cook for about 1 minute. Stir in the tomatoes and cook for about 2 minutes.

Meanwhile, in a small bowl, combine the ground cumin and coriander, garam masala and turmeric along with 2 tablespoons of water. Mix to a loose paste.

When the tomatoes have cooked, add the sugar and the spice mix and mix

well. Cook for about 4 minutes until the oils begin to release. At this point, add 100 ml (scant ½ cup) of water and bring to a simmer, then add the green chilli and salt, to taste.

Add a further 500 ml (2 cups) warm water and bring back to a simmer, then add the potatoes, reduce the heat, cover with a lid and cook for a further 10 minutes.

Check the potatoes are soft, then gently add the lentil cakes to the empty spaces in the pan, taking care not to overlap them so that they can absorb the gravy. Increase the heat to medium and cook for a further 3 minutes. Drizzle the ghee over the dish, remove from the heat and cover until ready to serve.

Bitter Gourd and Root Vegetable Medley

SHUKTO

4 tablespoons rapeseed (canola) oil

2 tablespoons *daaler bori* (dried urid lentil dumplings)

1 eggplant (aubergine), washed, skin on and cut into 1.5 cm (½ in) cubes

1 green banana, peeled and cut into 5 mm (¼ in) half-moons

1 bitter gourd (*korela*), washed and cut into 2.5 mm (⅛ in) discs

1 mooli (daikon), peeled and cut into 1.5 cm (½ in) cubes

50 g (2 oz) short flat green beans (*sheem*), topped and tailed, dethreaded and cut diagonally into thirds

1 moringa drumstick, dethreaded and cut into 3 cm (1 in) batons

1 tablespoon English mustard

2 teaspoons English mustard powder

2 teaspoons wholegrain mustard

1 teaspoon poppy seeds (optional)

2 teaspoons Paanch Phoron (page 218)

1 teaspoon celery seeds

2 bay leaves

1 potato, peeled and cut into 1.5 cm (½ in) cubes

1 Chinese okra/ridged gourd (*Jhinghe*), ridges peeled, skin removed and cut into 1.5 cm (½ in) cubes

5 cm (2 in) piece of fresh ginger, grated

1 teaspoon sugar

1 tablespoon ghee

salt, to taste

steamed rice, to serve

Shukto is traditionally eaten at the start of a Bengali lunch menu. It's considered a palate cleanser and also has health benefits because of the array of vegetables that are used, including the bitter gourd, which is highlighted in this dish. In *shukto* we also use something called *daal'er bori*, which are small sun-dried lentil dumplings. Bengalis are known for cooking with this unique ingredient – adding it to certain veg and fish dishes gives them a distinctive taste.

As a child, I wasn't keen on this dish, I think because of the slight bitterness, but I now find starting a meal with *shukto* and rice very appetising. I learned this recipe from my mother-in-law. There may be a number of unfamiliar vegetables here, but all can be sourced from Asian grocery stores.

Heat 1 tablespoon of the oil in a kadai or wok over a medium heat. When hot, gently add the lentil dumplings and fry until golden brown. Remove with a slotted spoon to a plate.

Using the same oil, repeat the process with the eggplant, green banana and bitter gourd. Place them all on the same plate after frying. (If the oil has reduced at any point, add another 1 tablespoon during the process.)

Bring a saucepan of salted water to the boil and gently add the mooli, green beans and moringa. Blanch for 2–3 minutes, then drain immediately, reserving 1 cup of the cooking water. Place the blanched vegetables on a separate plate and set aside. Let the reserved cooking water cool.

In a bowl, thoroughly combine the 3 mustards and the poppy seeds, then add the cup of cooled cooking water and mix again. Set aside.

Add the remaining 2–3 tablespoons of oil to the karai or wok and heat over a medium heat. Add the paanch phoron, celery seeds and bay leaves, letting them sizzle but not burn. Stir in the potato and cook for 4 minutes, stirring occasionally. Add the blanched vegetables and the Chinese okra/ ridged gourd, then continue to stir for a further 3 minutes. Add the ginger and sugar, cook for 2 minutes, then add the cooked eggplant and green banana. Continue to cook and stir for another 3 minutes, taking care not to mush the vegetables when stirring. Add the mustard water mixture, bring to the boil, then reduce the heat, season with salt to taste and cover. Simmer for 5 minutes until the vegetables are cooked through and a thick gravy has formed.

Sprinkle over the fried dumplings and bitter gourd, then delicately stir through just once.

Remove from the heat, drizzle over the ghee and cover until ready to serve.

Serve with steamed rice.

Shrimp with Poppy Seeds

CHINGRI POSTO

as a main serves
4

A dry-fry that is quick and easy to make as a weekday dinner. I learned this dish from my mother, who herself has fond memories of my grandmother making it. In Kolkata, freshly caught shrimp (prawns) were brought back from the fish market and within a couple of hours had been cooked and served for lunch. Eaten with steamed rice and a salad, it's perfect.

500 g (1 lb 2 oz) fresh raw shrimp (prawns), peeled and deveined

1 teaspoon salt, or to taste

1 teaspoon ground turmeric

3 tablespoons white poppy seeds

1 teaspoon black mustard seeds

2 teaspoons English mustard powder

1 tablespoon desiccated (dried unsweetened shredded) coconut (medium-size flakes)

1 tablespoon Greek-style yoghurt

1 teaspoon sugar

2 tablespoons mustard oil or rapeseed (canola) oil

1 potato, peeled and cut into 1 cm (½ in) cubes

1 bay leaf

½ teaspoon fenugreek seeds

1 white onion, finely chopped

2.5 cm (1 in) piece of fresh ginger, grated

1 dried red chilli

Put the shrimp in a bowl, add ½ teaspoon each of the salt and ground turmeric, and mix well to ensure all are coated. Set aside for 10 minutes.

Add the poppy and mustard seeds to a spice grinder and grind to a semi-coarse texture. Pour into a small bowl and combine with the English mustard powder, coconut, ½ tablespoon of the yoghurt, the remaining ½ teaspoon each of salt and turmeric, and ½ teaspoon of the sugar. Add 3 tablespoons of water and mix well to a paste. Set aside.

Heat about 1 tablespoon of the oil in a karai or wok over a medium heat. When hot, add the potatoes and cook for about 5 minutes until lightly browned, turning occasionally so they don't burn. Remove with a slotted spoon to a plate and set aside.

To the same pan, add the shrimp and sauté for about 2 minutes until they turn pink. Swiftly remove and return to their bowl.

Add the remaining oil to the pan, then add the bay leaf and fenugreek seeds.

Cook until the aromas release, then stir in the onions and cook for about 2 minutes. Add the remaining ½ teaspoon of sugar and continue to cook until the onions caramelise and become translucent. Add the ginger and dried chilli and cook for a further 2 minutes, stirring so the mixture doesn't stick to the pan.

Add the spice paste to the pan and stir well for about 3 minutes. Add the remaining ½ tablespoon of yoghurt and 150 ml (⅔ cup) warm water and bring to a simmer. Return the potatoes to the pan and bring back to a simmer. Check the seasoning and add more salt if desired.

Reduce the heat, cover and cook for 5–6 minutes. Check that the potatoes are cooked through and that the water has been absorbed. Stir in the shrimp, increase the heat and cook for a final 3–4 minutes until all the water has evaporated. Remove from the heat and cover until ready to serve.

Eggplant Fritters

BEGUNI

serves
4

Thelebhaja is a word that most Bengalis love to hear, and a word that many travelling to Kolkata discover, and then realise they love! It literally means 'fried in oil' and refers to many of the snacks that can be found on the street-corner stalls. A simple batter is made from gram flour, into which vegetables are dipped and then fried. The *beguni* is a very popular one, served in the evenings in a newspaper *thowa*,, a couple of *begunis* will be placed on top of some puffed rice with a couple of raw chillies. This dish is also served in family homes with *Kitchuri* (page 138) as a simple and wholesome meal.

2 eggplant (aubergines), washed and
    dried (try to find ones that aren't
    too thick in diameter)

2½ teaspoons salt

8 heaped tablespoons gram flour
    (besan)

2 heaped tablespoons rice flour

4 teaspoons nigella seeds

2 teaspoons white poppy seeds

2 teaspoons chilli powder

1 teaspoon ground turmeric

1 teaspoon baking powder

4 teaspoons mustard oil

vegetable oil, for frying

½ teaspoon black salt, to serve

Cut off the tops of the eggplant, then carefully cut them lengthways into slices, 5 mm (¼ in) thick. Place them on a plate and sprinkle them with ½ teaspoon of the salt. Leave to rest for 5 minutes to allow the salt to draw out excess moisture.

Meanwhile, combine the flours, nigella seeds, poppy seeds, chilli powder, turmeric, baking powder, mustard oil and the remaining salt in a large bowl. Mix gently with a spoon, then add 8 tablespoons of lukewarm water (the coating should not be too thick – add a little more water to make it into a semi-thin mixture, if needed). Mix well to ensure there are no lumps – you can whisk a little too as this allows some air to form in the mixture. Set aside.

Heat enough oil for frying in a frying pan (skillet) over a medium–high heat. I like to shallow-fry these.

Dab the excess moisture off the eggplant with some kitchen paper. Place each slice into the batter mixture, ensuring that both sides are coated (you will need to do this in batches).

When the oil is hot, carefully slide in each piece of batter-dipped eggplant to avoid splattering the hot oil (you will also need to do this in batches, possibly 2–3 slices at a time – don't overfill the pan). Cook on one side for about 2 minutes until the batter becomes a golden colour, then turn and cook the other sides. Remove from the oil with a slotted spoon to drain on kitchen paper. Repeat until all the slices are cooked.

Serve hot, sprinkled with the black salt, with steamed rice and dal (pages 33 or 49) or *Kitchuri* (page 138).

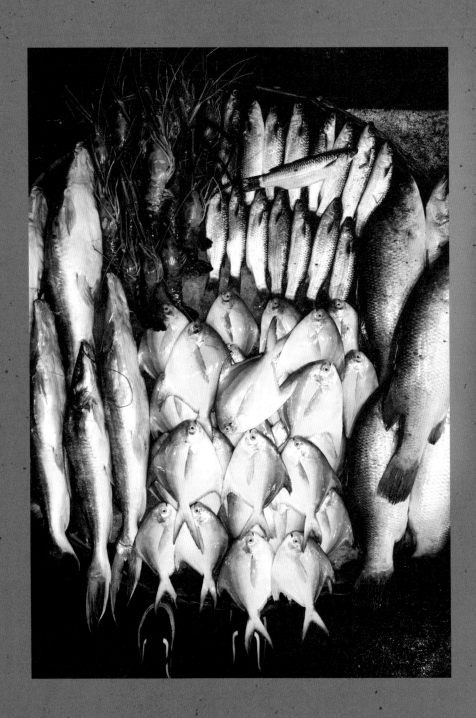

SNACKS

In Bengali cuisine, snacks come in various shapes and sizes, be they those made at home or those available in the many food stalls that line the streets. There are little nibbles, like the famous *chanachur* (Bengali Bombay mix) or *Chirey Bhaja* (page 83), or *Puchkas* (page 90); fingerfood, such as the various *chops* (pages 95 and 103) or *shingara* (pyramid-shaped pastries filled with different types of filling, similar to *samosa*); and more filling dishes, such as *Kati Rolls* (page 86) or Chilli Chicken (page 84). A Bengali neighbourhood is incomplete without a few little *singara*, or roll stalls. Whenever people would drop in to visit us unannounced, one of the family would be sent to run down and grab a few of these piping hot snacks from a stall and – boom – the impromtu *adda* would naturally be a superhit!

Adda is a term that has been associated with Bengali culture and daily life for centuries. One of our most beloved social activities, its formal definition is one of 'cultural osmosis'. It is the notion of several people gathering at a place, usually relaxed surroundings where one feels safe and comfortable to express oneself, and having a fluid discussion about anything. These *adda* can also include music, recitations, games and debates, but obviously food is an integral part of such gatherings. All food lovers acknowledge the fact that good food can be the element that turns a meeting of bonding, sharing and nostalgia into a state of magical perfection! The best part about an *adda* is that it can take place anywhere and at any time, in homes, cafés, streets... And, of course they can be planned or impromptu.

During my days in Kolkata, my love and appreciation for the city grew as I was introduced to the endless variety of simple but sumptuous street food. The more I discovered, the more I was inspired. The flavours and colours of Bengali street food are simply irresistible. In this chapter, I share recipes for snacks that are part of my beautiful memories, and I hope they become a part of your own, too.

Onion Fritters

PIYAJI

serves
4

Piyaji, also known as onion *pakoras*, are a gluten-free and a popular vegan street food dish. We would often walk down to the end of our lane around sunset, when our regular *thelebhaja* vendor would set up his stall and serve us fresh, irresistable *piyaji* in newspaper baskets. Using minimal ingredients, they can be served as a snack, starter or even with steamed rice and dal. *Piyaji* are popular all over India, with each region having their own slight variation to the recipe. The thickness of the onions are key to the crispiness of the *piyaji*. During our holidays in Kolkata, I can remember my grandmother quite often telling our cook off for cutting the onions too thick. I'm sharing my mother's recipe here, as it was passed down to her from her mother.

4 Bombay/white onions, halved and very thinly sliced

2 tablespoons finely chopped coriander (cilantro)

140 g (1¼ cups) gram flour (besan)

2 teaspoons nigella seeds

1 teaspoon chilli flakes

½ teaspoon baking powder

2 tablespoons Greek-style yoghurt

1½ teaspoons salt, or to taste

vegetable oil, for deep-frying

Place the sliced onions in a large mixing bowl and with clean hands gently separate all the strands. Add all the other ingredients, apart from the oil, and thoroughly mix with your hands to ensure the onions have been coated well. It will be a crumbly mixture. Set aside for 5 minutes for the water to release from the onions.

Meanwhile, heat enough oil for deep-frying in a karai or wok.

Add about 120 ml (½ cup) water to the onion mixture and gently mix with your fingers until all the lumps disappear and a thick mixture has formed.

When the oil is hot, carefully slide in a tablespoonful of the onion batter. It should immediately start bubbling and rise to the top. Add just a few *piyajis* at a time so the pan does not become overcrowded. Fry on one side for about 2 minutes until golden brown, then turn and cook the other sides, keeping a close eye on them so they don't burn. Remove with a slotted spoon to drain on kitchen paper. Repeat with the rest of the mixture.

Serve and enjoy freshly fried.

Crispy Rice and Lentil Mix

CHIREY BHAJA

I often think of *chirey bhaja* as a Bengali version of Bombay mix. With flattened rice and skinned peanuts as the main ingredients, we usually make this in batches that stay fresh for over a week. It pairs perfectly with tea as a late afternoon/early evening light snack and many people have it on their return from work, while they wait for dinner to be made. I always have a jar of this at home, as it makes it an interesting alternative to serving crisps.

6 tablespoons Bengal gram lentils (channa dal)

2 tablespoons rapeseed (canola) oil

4 tablespoons whole redskin peanuts

3 dried red chillies

25 curry leaves

1 teaspoon black mustard seeds

200 g (scant 2 cups) medium pounded rice (you may find this sold as 'rice flakes' or under any of the following names: chira/chirey/ poha/powa/pawa)

1 tablespoon demerara sugar

½ teaspoon black salt

½ teaspoon asafoetida

¼ teaspoon red chilli powder

½ teaspoon amchur (mango) powder

½ teaspoon salt, or to taste

Preheat the oven to 180°C (350°F/gas 4).

Place the lentils in a saucepan and rinse a couple of times until the water is nearly clear. Cover with fresh water and leave to soak for 30 minutes. Once soaked, bring to a simmer over a medium heat. Skim off and discard the foam that rises to the surface. Boil for about 5 minutes, then drain.

Spread the lentils over a shallow baking tray, drizzle with ½ tablespoon of the oil and ½ teaspoon of salt and toss, ensuring the lentils are well coated. Roast in the oven for 25 minutes, stirring with a wooden spoon every 10 minutes to make sure the lentils don't burn. Remove and set aside to cool.

Heat ½ tablespoon of the oil in a karai or wok over a medium heat. When hot, add the peanuts and fry for about 4 minutes, stirring continuously, until they turn a rich maroon colour. Remove with a slotted spoon to a bowl lined with kitchen paper to drain.

To the same oil, add the chillies and curry leaves. Allow them to crackle and the chillies to blister slightly for 2 minutes, then remove to the same bowl as the peanuts.

Add the remaining tablespoon of oil to the pan. When hot, add the mustard seeds, then the pounded rice. Cook for about 5 minutes, stirring to ensure the rice doesn't turn brown, until the rice is cooked and crispy. Stir very gently as the rice will break if handled with too much force. Once the rice is cooked, add the remaining ingredients, stir and season to taste.

Remove from the heat and spread over a large tray. Add the peanuts, chillies, curry leaves and roasted lentils, lightly toss together and leave to cool.

When cool, enjoy immediately or store in an airtight container.

Indo-Chinese Chicken

CHILLI CHICKEN

serves
4

500 g (1 lb 2 oz) skinless and boneless chicken thighs, cut into 2.5 cm (1 in) cubes

rapeseed (canola) oil, for deep-frying

For the marinade

1 white onion, roughly chopped

5 cm (2 in) piece of fresh ginger, peeled and cut into quarters

4 garlic cloves

2 tablespoons dark soy sauce

1 tablespoon lemon juice

½ teaspoon baking powder

1 teaspoon black pepper

1 egg

1 tablespoon Chinese cooking wine

2 teaspoons cornflour (cornstarch)

For the coating

4 heaped tablespoons cornflour (cornstarch)

4 heaped tablespoons plain (all-purpose) flour

½ teaspoon salt

For the gravy

3 tablespoons rapeseed (canola) oil

6 garlic cloves, finely chopped

3 bird's eye chillies, slit lengthways

2 red onions, halved, then each half quartered to make chunky square pieces

1 green bell pepper (capsicum), deseeded, coarsely chopped

1 red bell pepper (capsicum), deseeded, coarsely chopped

2 tablespoons dark soy sauce

2 tablespoons light soy sauce

3 tablespoons tomato ketchup

2 tablespoons sweet chilli sauce

1 tablespoon chopped coriander (cilantro) (optional)

Kolkata is well known for its multicultural community. The Chinese settled during the 18th century and have had a large influence on food in the city. The fusion of Indian and Chinese foods (Indo-Chinese cuisine) occupies a major space in the street food and restaurant scene. Tangra is the place to find it.

We make this delicious snack when we have *addas* at home. An *adda* – a gathering of friends and family for relaxing – is an important part of the Kolkata lifestyle. Sometimes impromptu and other times planned, they will almost always feature food: snacks with drinks, nibbles with tea, and often a meal. Chilli chicken works well on its own as a snack, but we also serve it with *hakka* noodles and chillies in vinegar for a main.

Start with the marinade. Put the onion, ginger and garlic into a blender, add 2 tablespoons of water and blend to a thick, semi-smooth paste. Transfer to a large bowl and add the remaining marinade ingredients along with the chicken. Mix well, ensuring all the ingredients have coated the chicken. Cover and refrigerate for a minimum of 2 hours, but ideally overnight.

Once marinated, bring the chicken to room temperature for 40 minutes.

Combine the coating ingredients on a plate and mix well. Set aside.

In a karai or wok, heat enough oil for deep-frying.

Meanwhile, take a piece of chicken out of the marinade and place it in the coating mixture. Press quite firmly, so it is well but thinly coated. Try not to get too much flour on each piece otherwise it will make the gravy too thick. Place on a plate and repeat until all the chicken pieces are coated.

When the oil is hot, carefully lower a few pieces of chicken at a time into the oil and fry for about 3 minutes until golden brown. Remove with a slotted spoon to a plate. Repeat with all the remaining pieces.

In a separate pan, make the gravy. Heat the oil over a medium heat, add the garlic and stir for 30 seconds, taking care not to burn it. Add the chillies and onions, and continue to stir-fry for 1 minute. Add the peppers, increase the heat to high, and cook for 2 minutes. Add all of the sauces, mix well and cook for 1 minute, then add the fried chicken pieces. Gently stir to ensure the chicken pieces are well coated with the gravy, then reduce the heat to medium and cook for a further 4 minutes, stirring occasionally.

If desired, sprinkle the chopped coriander over the chilli chicken and serve immediately.

Kolkata-Style Egg Roll

EGG KATI ROLL

serves
4

For the *porota*

300 g (scant 2½ cups) plain (all-purpose) flour, plus extra for dusting

½ teaspoon salt

¼ teaspoon sugar

1 teaspoon butter

about 120 ml (½ cup) lukewarm water

4 eggs

1 teaspoon cumin seeds

sea salt, to taste

2 tablespoons rapeseed (canola) oil

For the fillings

½ cucumber, julienned

1 red onion, finely sliced

2 chillies, finely chopped

½ lime, for squeezing

1 tablespoon rapeseed (canola) oil

1 teaspoon cumin seeds

½ white onion, finely chopped

1 teaspoon sugar

400 g (14 oz) tin of chickpeas (garbanzo beans), drained

1 tomato, roughly chopped

1 teaspoon grated fresh ginger

1 teaspoon grated garlic

½ teaspoon ground turmeric

1 teaspoon ground cumin

1 teaspoon ground coriander

1 teaspoon dried fenugreek leaves

1 teaspoon salt

1 teaspoon Greek-style yoghurt

½ teaspoon mint sauce

1 teaspoon tamarind sauce (store-bought)

1 teaspoon *Pudina Chutney* (page 213)

½ teaspoon black salt

fresh herbs, for sprinkling

The first *kati roll* was made in Nizam's, an eatery that is still going strong in Kolkata, and a place that tourists will make a point of going to visit. For every Kolkatan Bengali, the egg roll holds a special place. It is a simple yet filling street-food dish that was traditionally bought by workers on their way home from work as a tummy filler. Now, tourists from all over the world seek to try (and re-try) one when they are in the city.

Another place that is now famous for *kati roll* is Kusum. The sheer experience of watching your roll being made is one to remember. In their work area, they have hundreds of pre-made *porota* dough balls, that upon each order are rolled out and cooked fresh, then filled with your choice of fillings and sauces – all made and served to you in a matter of seconds.

This dish was one of the main inspirations behind opening our street-food van, Raastawala. We wanted people in London to be able to experience this unique street food. Although any flatbread can be used to make a *kati roll*, in this recipe we will make a *porota*, just like they make on the streets of Kolkata. Traditionally, the roll is filled with chicken cubes, or even double egg *kati rolls* can be requested, with shredded onion, cucumber and tomato ketchup. Further fillings of marinated meats and veg can also be added. It can be served for lunch, dinner or as a snack. In this recipe, I have added a chickpea (garbanzo bean) filling, as the combination works really well together.

To make the *porota*, combine the flour, salt, sugar and butter in a medium bowl and mix well to a fine breadcrumb texture. Slowly add half of the water and knead into a soft dough, adding extra water if required. The dough should be soft and bouncy. Cover with a damp dish towel and leave to rest for 25 minutes.

For the filling, place the cucumber, onions and chillies in a bowl, squeeze over some of the lime juice and mix. Leave to pickle.

Once the dough has rested, divide into 4 equal portions. Dust the work surface with some flour and roll out the dough balls into flat discs, about 15 cm (6 in) in diameter. Slit each disc from the middle to the edge, then roll them into cone shapes. Squeeze between your palms to flatten the cones from the top to the bottom, then leave to rest for 10 minutes. Once rested, roll each piece out to a 15–17 cm (6–6½ in) round.

Method continues overleaf

While the dough is resting, make the other fillings. Heat the oil in a small pan over a medium heat. Add the cumin seeds and allow to crackle, then add the chopped white onion and the sugar, and cook, stirring, for 2 minutes. Add the chickpeas, tomato, ginger and garlic, stir well and cook for 4 minutes. Add the ground spices and fenugreek, stir to coat the chickpeas and cook for 4 minutes. Add 150 ml (generous ½ cup) water and bring to a simmer. Add the salt, reduce the heat, cover and cook for a further 8 minutes. Remove the lid and check that the water has evaporated to form a dry gravy. If there is excess liquid, increase the heat and allow the water to evaporate. Set aside.

In a small bowl, mix together the yoghurt and mint sauce. Set aside.

Return to the *porota*. Crack one of the eggs into a separate bowl and whisk with a pinch of sea salt. Heat a medium frying pan (skillet) over a high heat. Add ½ tablespoon of the oil and heat for 1 minute, then place a *porota* in the pan and cook until golden spots appear. Flip and cook on the other side until golden. Sprinkle a pinch of the cumin seeds over the *porota*, then pour over the beaten egg and flip the *porota* again. The egg will now be under the *porota*. Keep pressing down on it to ensure that both the bread and the egg are fully cooked. Remove and wrap in foil while you cook the rest of the *porota* and eggs.

To serve, place a sheet of greaseproof paper on a plate and top with a *porota*. Spoon a line of the chickpea filling down the middle, add a line of the salad followed by another squeeze of lime juice. Drizzle with tamarind sauce, mint chutney and the yoghurt raita. Sprinkle with a pinch of black salt and some fresh herbs. Roll up using the paper to help you, twisting the sheet at the end to enclose. Repeat for all the *porota* and serve hot.

Spicy Water Bombs

PUCHKAS

For the *puris* (puffs)

130g (1 cup) fine semolina flour

¼ teaspoon baking powder

1 tablespoon plain (all-purpose) flour, plus extra for dusting

¼ teaspoon salt

60ml (¼ cup) sparkling water

rapeseed (canola) oil, for deep-frying

For the filling

1 x 400g (14oz) tin of black chickpeas (kala chana)

3 waxy potatoes, peeled and cut into very small cubes

1 red onion, very finely chopped

1 green chilli (add more to increase heat level)

3 tablespoons chaat masala (available in Asian grocers of the spice aisle of your supermarket)

1 teaspoon salt

2 tablespoons finely chopped coriander (cilantro)

1 tablespoon rapeseed (canola) oil

For the tamarind water (makes about 100 ml/scant ½ cup)

4 tablespoons tamarind paste (good-quality, with no fibre strands)

3 tablespoons jaggery or any dark sugar

1 teaspoon chilli powder

1 teaspoon Jeera Bhaja Masala (see page 218)

½ teaspoon salt

8 tablespoons water

Semolina puffs (*puris*) with spiced potatoes and tamarind water – this incredible snack can be found on every street corner in Kolkata. Keen *puchka*-lovers are known to compete with each other to see who can devour the most in the fastest time possible. These puffs can be enjoyed any time of the day, as a snack, lunch or even a starter. Every household has their version of the recipe, and mine comes from my parents, who have used it to entertain loved ones for decades. At Raastawala, we serve them at our supper clubs and call them 'spicy water bombs' to reflect the sheer explosion of flavours. To save time, you can skip making the *puris* and buy them ready-made in Asian food stores.

For the *puris*, combine the semolina, baking powder, flour, salt and water in a bowl. Knead for about 10 minutes, ensuring the dough is quite tough and all the water has been absorbed. Form into a ball, cover with a dish towel and leave to rest for 15 minutes.

Divide the dough into 8 balls of equal size. On a flour-dusted work surface, roll out each ball to 1–2 mm (¹⁄₁₆ in) thick. From each piece, press out 4 discs of dough with a round pastry cutter or jar lid, about 4 cm (1½ in) in diameter, until you have 32 little discs.

Heat enough oil for deep-frying in a deep pan. Check that it is hot enough by adding a piece of spare dough to the oil. If it rises to the top, the oil is ready. Carefully place the *puris* into the oil, no more than 3 or 4 at a time. Once they puff into a ball, immediately remove with a slotted spoon to drain on kitchen paper. Repeat until all are cooked and leave to cool.

For the filling, place the potatoes in a saucepan and cover with water. Bring to the boil and simmer for 10 minutes, then drain and cool.

Combine the remaining ingredients for the filling in a bowl and mix well. Mix in the potatoes when cool.

For the tamarind water, place all the ingredients in a saucepan, mix well and bring to the boil. Simmer for about 5 minutes until thick, then remove from the heat and cool. (When cool, this tamarind chutney can be refrigerated for up to 2 weeks to use as needed.) Dilute the chutney in a small jug with 2 parts water: 1 part chutney. Mix well.

Assemble the dish just before serving, otherwise the *puris* will become soggy. Take each *puri* and gently knock a hole into the middle of one side with the back of a teaspoon. Add 1 teaspoon of the filling mixture to each *puri*. Serve with the tamarind water on the side. To eat, pour about 2 teaspoons of tamarind water into a *puri* and immediately pop it into your mouth.

Bengali Fish Croquettes

MACHER CHOP

serves 4

These spiced fish croquettes, served with a carrot and beet pickle and *Kasundi* (mustard relish, see page 214), make a perfect starter for any dinner party or are delicious simply devoured with a drink as a snack.

Macher chop is a popular street food. Street vendors pile them high on each side of the cart, and a small circular iron flat plate in the middle. As orders come in, a vendor simply takes a couple of chops and some oil, and gently heats them. They are served up in 2 minutes.

The beauty of this versatile dish is that it can be cooked with any type of white fish. In this recipe, I have used tinned tuna.

1 potato, peeled and cut into medium cubes

2 tablespoons canola (rapeseed) oil

1 small white onion, finely chopped

½ teaspoon sugar

1 garlic clove, finely grated

2 x 145 g (5 oz) tins of tuna chunks in brine or sunflower oil, drained

1 teaspoon ground cumin

2 teaspoons Barir Bhaja Masala (page 218)

1 green bird's eye chilli, finely chopped

2 tablespoons chopped coriander (cilantro), leaves and stalks

2 eggs

fine golden breadcrumbs, for coating

salt, to taste

oil, for deep-frying

For the pickle

1 carrot, peeled

1 beetroot (beet), peeled

½ teaspoon salt

juice of ½ lime

Begin with the pickle. Cut the carrot and beetroot into very fine strips, each about 4 cm (1½ in) long and 3 mm (⅛ in) thick. Place in separate bowls to avoid the beet colour running into the carrot. Add ¼ teaspoon of salt and half of the lime juice to each bowl. Mix and set aside for at least an hour. Mix the carrot and beet together only just before you are ready to serve.

Fill a saucepan halfway with boiling water and set over a medium heat. Add a pinch of salt, then add the potato and boil for 7–8 minutes until soft. Drain immediately and set aside.

In a karai or wok, heat the oil over a medium heat, add the onions and sauté for 2 minutes before adding the sugar. Cook until the onions are translucent. Add the garlic and cook for 1 minute. Add the tuna and stir to break up the chunks with a wooden spoon. Mix in the cumin and 1½ teaspoons of the bhaja masala, then add the chilli and coriander. Stir well and season to taste. Remove from the heat and let cool.

When cool, add the fish mixture to the bowl of cooled potatoes along with the remaining ½ teaspoon of bhaja masala. Mash together with a fork or clean hands for about 5 minutes, ensuring everything is well combined. Divide the mixture into 12 equal portions and shape each one into an oblong shape with smooth sides.

Whisk the eggs in a bowl. Sprinkle a thick layer of breadcrumbs over a flat plate. With clean, dry hands take a croquette in your right hand and roll gently in the breadcrumbs. Transfer the croquette to your left hand and gently place it in the egg, rolling it until well coated. With your left hand, place it back into the breadcrumbs, then roll with your right hand until evenly but thinly coated. Place on a plate and repeat until all the croquettes are coated.

Heat enough oil for deep-frying in a karai or wok over a medium heat. When the oil is hot, carefully lower a few croquettes into the oil. Fry for about 3 minutes until golden brown all over. Remove with a slotted spoon to drain on kitchen paper. Repeat until all are fried.

Serve with the pickle in a small bowl on the side with some *kasundi* relish (page 214) for dipping.

Crunchy Savoury Chai-Time Snacks

NIMKI

makes **1** large jar

Offer someone from Kolkata some *nimki* and a cup of chai and sure enough they won't refuse! These remind me of monsoon afternoons at home with friends, with the sound of smashing raindrops and the smell of the monsoon earth, sitting on the swing in our balcony, watching passers-by rush for shelter and the yellow taxis being halted for pick-ups. The tea would be bubbling away in a saucepan with aromatic spices and freshly made *nimki* would make the perfect snack accompaniment.

450 g (1 lb/4 cups) plain (all-purpose) flour

2 teaspoons nigella seeds

½ teaspoon caraway seeds

1½ teaspoons salt

½ teaspoon sugar

2 tablespoons ghee

water, for kneading

vegetable oil, for greasing and deep-frying

Combine the flour, nigella and caraway seeds, salt, sugar and ghee in a medium mixing bowl. Mix with your fingers to form a crumbly dough. Gradually add small amounts of water and continue kneading until a smooth dough forms. It should be soft yet holding together firmly. Cover with a damp dish towel and leave to rest for 40 minutes.

Once rested, divide the dough into 6 equal-sized balls.

On a clean work surface, spread a thin layer of oil. Flatten a ball on the work surface and use a rolling pin to roll it out to 2 mm (1/16 in) thick. With a sharp knife cut the circle into diamond shapes. Each diamond should be about 1.5 cm (½ in) wide. Re-roll the scraps until all the dough is used up.

Heat enough oil for deep-frying in a karai or wok. To test when it is hot enough, add one piece of the dough – it should bubble and rise to the top of the oil. When hot enough, slowly lower the diamonds into the oil in batches. Take care not to put too many diamonds in at once. Cook for about 2 minutes until golden brown. Remove with a slotted spoon to drain on kitchen paper.

Repeat the process with the remaining balls of dough.

Enjoy the *nimki* when freshly made with a cup of tea. Alternatively, they can be cooled and stored in an airtight container for up to 2 weeks.

Savoury Spiced Puffed Rice Mix

JHAL MURI

serves 4

Traditionally served in a *thonga*, which is a small basket made of newspaper, *jhal muri* is a very popular street food snack readily available at most street corners in Kolkata. The main ingredient is *muri*, which is puffed rice, and this brings the dish together. It is quite complex in taste, yet light and refreshing too. My memories of this go back to my childhood days, when I would visit my paternal grandparents' home, and the *muriwala* would push his old wooden cart round outside the house, shouting '*muri, jhal muri, jhal jhal muri*'. I remember the sheer excitement of running down the marble staircase in my noisiest flip-flops to reach his cart. The *jhal muri* was quite spicy, but was so tasty that I couldn't resist!

Back home in London, my parents would often try to replicate this as a Sunday afternoon snack, and as few Indian ingredients could be sourced here, they would use Rice Krispies as a substitute. Surprisingly, it worked really well. I serve this dish as a starter at my supperclubs now. The puffed rice can be found in most Asian grocery stores.

1 small potato, peeled and cut into 1 cm (½ in) cubes

3 tablespoons store-bought Bombay mix

1 tablespoon whole redskin peanuts

½ small red onion, finely chopped

1 cm (½ in) piece of fresh ginger, grated

1 green bird's eye chilli, finely chopped

½ teaspoon black salt

½ teaspoon chaat masala

2 tablespoons finely chopped cucumber

1 tablespoon finely chopped coriander (cilantro)

1 cup puffed rice (*muri*)

1 tablespoon mustard oil

Bring a small saucepan of salted water to the boil over a medium heat. Add the potato and boil for about 6 minutes until soft but not falling apart. Drain and set aside to cool.

Combine all the ingredients, apart from the potatoes, puffed rice and mustard oil, in a mixing bowl and mix well. Finally, add these last three ingredients and mix well.

Serve immediately, otherwise it will get soggy.

Street Food

Street food is a way of life in Kolkata. Pretty much every street corner has a food vendor of some kind, calling out for new customers while busily serving the existing ones who are standing around the stall. The dishes are often made from very simple ingredients, but the combination of them is always delicious. The food is also very cheap, so everyone can afford to enjoy it.

Although street food can be found at any time of the day, between lunch and dinner are the magic hours when the street vendors really come to life. From the *telebhaja* stands, where all sorts of vegetables are thinly sliced, dipped in gram flour and deep-fried, to the bright yellow *chaat* counters, mixing up that sweet, sour and spicy concoction of ingredients to serve up the most delicious *chaats* in town, to the *puckhawala*, with his heaped mountain of *puchka* and stainless-steel bowls with the delicious filling and container of spicy water, the list of options is endless.

Local residents get well acquainted with their local vendors and it is always something special when the vendor remembers you and makes the dish according to your liking. My favourite was the *puchka* stand, a cart on wheels that the *puchkawala* would park at the corner of my grandmother's home every day from about 6 pm to serve his local fans – always with a smile! He got to know that I liked my *puchka* filling with extra spice, and that's exactly how he would prepare it as soon as I walked towards his cart.

Many dishes reflect the rich diversity of cultures and communities that have settled in Kolkata over the years, such as the *hakka* noodles originating from the Chinese community, which is the largest in India. Also, the fish fry served with *kasundi*, which can be found in many street stalls, is the Kolkatan take on British breaded fish, an overhang from colonial times. Nepalese *momos* are another much-loved street food in Kolkata. The *momo* stalls with massive round steamers layered on top of each other are a lovely sight to see.

There are also many 'hole in the wall' businesses selling street food. The little nooks and crannies where food sellers set up is so fun to see – necessity and invention is all around you in the city. Kusum is one such place, situated on Park Street, famous for their *kati rolls* and visited by customers all through the day and night. The menu is quite vast, ranging from a simple porota with a single egg to one with a triple egg layer and double meat filling, with red onions, chillies and sauces – an extremely delicious, rich snack.

The ability of these Kolkatan vendors to transform a few mundane ingredients into a mouth-watering snack never ceases to amaze me. There are *chaats* made of potatoes and chickpeas (garbanzo beans); Bengali beetroot (beet) *chops*; *churmur* made out of crumbled crunchy *puchka* cases, drizzled with sweet yoghurt, tangy tamarind sauce and chilli sauce. The balance of flavours and spices in these morsels is almost always perfect.

When my husband Neelan and I decided to have our Indian wedding in Kolkata, we wanted it to be a grand affair, so we hired a *rajbari* (a Hindu royal residence). We had guests flying in from all parts of the world and we wanted them to experience an authentic wedding with all the rituals, but also a culinary feast. As part of the starters for the wedding feast, we had Kolkatan street food stalls set up on the lawn, where guests could go and order personalised dishes made to their request. To this day, our friends still talk about the street food stalls, as they enjoyed them so much!

Bengali Devilled Egg Chops

DIMER DEVIL

serves
4

4 large eggs

2 potatoes, peeled and cubed

2 tablespoons rapeseed (canola) oil

1 small onion, finely chopped

1 teaspoon sugar

3 garlic cloves, grated

1 cm (½ in) piece of fresh ginger, grated

200 g (7 oz) minced (ground) lamb (10% fat)

1 teaspoon ground turmeric

2 teaspoons ground coriander

2 teaspoons ground cumin

2 teaspoons Bengali Garam Masala (page 218)

1 teaspoon chilli powder

1 teaspoon salt, or to taste

1 green bird's eye chilli, very finely chopped

1 tablespoon finely chopped coriander (cilantro)

1½ teaspoons Barir Bhaja Masala (page 218)

To finish

2 eggs

2 handfuls of fine golden breadcrumbs

vegetable oil, for deep-frying

To serve

Kasundi (mustard relish, see page 214)

finely sliced carrots, beetroot (beets) and red onion

Often referred to as a relative of the Scotch egg, *dimer devil* is thought to have originated back in colonial times. The 'devilling' of a dish is when it's spiced up and this is definitely that! A labour of love, *dimer devil* involves a few stages of cooking, but is absolutely delicious and usually disappears in an instant. Traditionally, the *dimer devil* is a hard-boiled egg, halved, wrapped in a spiced potato mash, then coated with golden breadcrumbs. My parents would elevate this when hosting dinner parties and add some lamb keema to the potato mix. I remember getting involved in the careful coating of the eggs, with the art of using the right 'dry hand' for the breadcrumbs and the left 'wet hand' for the egg mixture. This was to avoid lumps and a messy coating. This recipe holds a special place, for me and everyone I serve it to!

Hard-boil the eggs for 9 minutes, then transfer to a bowl of cold water to cool.

To the same pan, add the potatoes and top up with boiling water to cover. Gently boil for about 5 minutes until soft but not mushy. Drain and set aside to cool. When cool, mash until smooth.

Heat the oil in a frying pan (skillet) over a medium heat. When hot, add the onions and sugar and cook until gently browned. Add the garlic and ginger, cook for 2 minutes, then stir in the lamb. Add the ground turmeric, coriander, cumin, garam masala, chilli powder and salt. Cook, stirring, for

5 minutes, then cover and cook for a further 5 minutes. Transfer the mixture to a large bowl and leave to cool.

When cool, add the mashed potatoes, chopped fresh chilli, coriander and bhaja masala, and mix until very well combined. Taste and check the seasoning, then set aside.

Gently peel the cooled hard-boiled eggs, then halve each egg vertically with a sharp knife. Take a small amount of the potato and lamb mixture and form it into a shape that matches the other half of an egg. Gently pair half an egg together with it, then take a little more potato mixture and form it around the egg half to make a smooth

Method continues overleaf

oval. Place on a plate and repeat with the other egg halves and potato mixture. Place in the refrigerator for 30 minutes to firm up.

To coat the ovals, remove from the fridge and set to one side. Whisk the eggs in a small bowl and place it on your left. Spread out the breadcrumbs on a wide plate and set it to your right. Lay out an empty plate nearby. With your right hand, take an oval and gently roll it in the breadcrumbs. Still using your right hand, lower the coated oval into the egg wash, taking care not to get any wet mixture on your right hand. Use your left hand to ensure the oval is fully coated with the egg wash. With this hand, place the oval back on the breadcrumbs, making sure you don't get any

breadcrumbs on the 'wet hand'. Use your right hand to roll the oval shape in the breadcrumbs until it is fully coated. (You may need to repeat this process to get it well coated.) Place on the empty plate and repeat the process until all are coated.

Heat enough oil for deep-frying in a karai or wok. When hot, carefully place a few ovals into the oil and fry for about 4 minutes until golden. Take care not to place too many in at once, otherwise they may break. Remove with a slotted spoon to drain on kitchen paper. Repeat until all are cooked.

Serve immediately with *kasundi*, finely sliced carrots, beets and red onions.

EVENING DINNER

The evening meal, or *raat'er kabher*, is is usually lighter than lunch (unless you have guests over or it's a special occasion – for those recipes, see the Family Feasts and Festive Meals chapter, page 130). Sitting around the table after a hard day's work, talking, laughing and sometimes even squabbling is part of everyday life. Yet it is common practice to eat late in Kolkata, often at 9 or 10 pm, so when most people come back from school or work, they will have a substantial snack to see them through for a few hours until the main meal.

It is quite normal for most middle-class families to have a cook come to the house for a few hours every morning to make meals for the day. Breakfast, lunch and the *torkari* and dals for dinner are made ahead of time, then reheated when it's time to eat. The cook will usually return again in the evening to make fresh *rooti* or rice to eat with dinner. Historically, it was common for the lady of the house to serve food to the other members of the family and only sit down to have her meal after everyone had finished. My grandmother would recount tales of her mother's generation, where the ladies of the house would stand around their grand dining table serving the dishes they had prepared. Thankfully, nowadays, everyone sits together and serves themselves.

The recipes in this chapter are some of the more traditional home-cooked dinners found in many households across Kolkata. I have included dishes that were made at home when I was a child and ones I relish preparing for my family now. Some dishes, such as the *Shorshey maach* (page 116), have been adapted to being oven-baked or cooked under the grill (broiler), while retaining the classic flavours.

In Kolkata, the most affordable and commonly eaten fish is *ruhi*, white and fleshy with relatively few bones. Steamed or fried, it is then cooked in a *jhol* (sauce) or deep-fried. All parts of this large carp are cooked – the head is cooked in a dry-fry with potatoes and is a classic Bengali dish. The other fish relished by Bengalis is the *hilsa* or *ilish maach*. Sometimes called the 'king of fishes', this oily and distinct-flavoured fish is a delicacy in West Bengal. Available in monsoon season, it is very expensive, so it tends to be eaten on special occasions. All the fish dishes in this chapter can be cooked with either *ruhi* or *ilish*, but as they can be tricky to get hold of, I've suggested salmon, which tastes incredible too.

Red Lentil Dal

MASOOR DAL

serves
4

This is a classic Bengali *masoor dal* – although commonly found in restaurants, my experience is that home-cooked ones are the most satisfying. The secret of this dal is the simplicity of it and the fact that it is not rich at all. It's an everyday staple in many households, eaten with rice for lunch and enjoyed with *rooti* (page 197) in the evening. This was one of the first dishes I learned to cook from my father and weekends would be spent watching both my parents cook it for the guests that evening. I'm sharing his recipe here, as to me it's still the best!

100 g (generous ½ cup) red split lentils (masoor dal)

1 white onion, finely chopped

3 garlic cloves, finely chopped

1 tomato, roughly chopped

1 teaspoon ground turmeric

1½ tablespoons ghee

1½ teaspoons nigella seeds

1 whole dried red chilli

salt, to taste

boiled rice or *Rooti* (page 197), to serve

In a heavy-based pan, wash the lentils thoroughly under running water, using your hands to filter them. Repeat at least twice until the water is clear.

Top up the pan with fresh water to a depth of 2.5 cm (1 in) above the lentils. Place over a medium heat and bring to a simmer. Gently skim off and discard any foam that forms.

Add half of the chopped onion, half of the chopped garlic, the chopped tomatoes and ground turmeric, and mix well. When the dal starts to bubble, reduce the heat to low, cover with a lid and simmer for a further 10 minutes.

Check that the lentils have become soft but still with a little texture and that the mixture has thickened. If not, cook for another 5 minutes until the desired consistency is reached. Keep over a low heat while you make the temper.

To make the temper, place a small frying pan (skillet) over a medium heat. Add the ghee and allow to melt, then add the nigella seeds and dried chilli. Cook until the aromas release but take care not to burn the spices. Add the remaining onions and garlic and keep stirring until the garlic is slightly browned and the onions are translucent.

Increase the heat under the dal to medium, then carefully add the temper to the pan. Mix well. Add salt to taste and continue to simmer for a further 3 minutes.

Remove from the heat and cover the pan until ready to serve.

Pour into a serving dish and serve with boiled rice or *rooti*, or both.

Eggplant and Spinach Dry-Fry

BEGUN SHAAK

A no-waste policy has always been an integral part of the Bengali culinary scene. The importance of using all parts of produce is taken very seriously (be it vegetable peelings or fish heads) and some of dishes that have been discovered as a result are among the finest, for example the variety of *shaak*, which often make use of the leaves of whatever vegetable is to be cooked that evening. *Shaak* are edible leaves that are cooked in simple whole spices and condensed down so all the water is evaporated. A *shaak* is eaten to start a Bengali meal, very much like *Shukto* (page 69) – you will have a tablespoon of it along with some plain boiled white rice. My mother mostly used spinach. Once in a while, if my father got some *lal shaak* (red leaves/amaranth) at the Asian grocers, that would be a treat, as our rice would turn pink when we mixed them together!

1 eggplant (aubergine), cut into 1 cm (½ in) cubes

½ teaspoon ground turmeric

1 tablespoon mustard oil or rapeseed (canola) oil

1 teaspoon Paanch Phoron (page 218)

1 dried red chilli

300 g (10½ oz) baby spinach, washed and drained

½ teaspoon ghee

salt, to taste

steamed rice, to serve

Spread the cubed eggplant over a large plate and sprinkle with the turmeric and ½ teaspoon of salt. With clean hands, mix the cubes gently so that the eggplant is well coated and set aside for 10 minutes. After this time, use a piece of kitchen paper to gently press on the eggplant so that any excess water is absorbed.

In a shallow frying pan (skillet), heat ½ tablespoon of the oil over a medium heat. When hot, add the eggplant and cook for 5–6 minutes until soft and browned on all sides. Take care not to stir too much, otherwise the cubes may start to break up. Remove from the pan to a plate.

Add the remaining ½ tablespoon of oil to the same pan, then add the paanch phoron and chilli. When the aromas have released, add the baby spinach and stir well. Eventually, the spinach will begin to wilt and water will be released. Add salt to taste and continue to cook for 7–8 minutes until all the water has evaporated. Return the eggplant to the pan and stir to combine. The mixture should be dry with no excess water. Remove from the heat and add the ghee, then cover until ready to serve.

Serve with steamed rice.

Bengali Fish Curry

MAACHER JHOL

serves 4

Any cookbook about Kolkata would be incomplete without this recipe. For Bengalis, rice and fish represent a love affair on a plate. As a city on a bay, Kolkata is lucky to have the freshest fish every morning. The wet fish markets are quite a scene to experience and the huge variety of fish on offer can be overwhelming. The most common, everyday fish is the *ruhi*, or *katla*, a meaty white fish.

This dish is traditionally cooked with *ruhi*, but as it isn't easily sourced outside India, I use salmon fillets, which deliver just as tasty a *maacher jhol*. I was brought up eating this version, as going to the East End of London to buy frozen *ruhi* wasn't always convenient – we saved those trips for when we had special guests!

4 salmon fillets, skin on and scaled, boneless if possible

2 teaspoons ground turmeric

2 potatoes, peeled and cut into long chunky strips

1 small eggplant (aubergine), skin-on, cut into long chunky strips

3 tablespoons mustard oil or rapeseed (canola) oil

2 teaspoons cumin seeds

1 bay leaf

1 white onion, finely chopped

½ teaspoon sugar

2.5 cm (1 in) piece of fresh ginger, grated

1 green bird's eye chilli, slit lengthways

2 tomatoes, roughly chopped

1 teaspoon ground cumin

1 handful of coriander (cilantro) leaves

salt, to taste

To serve

steamed rice

lemon wedges

Lay the salmon fillets on a plate and sprinkle with ½ teaspoon of the turmeric and a pinch of salt, rubbing them in well so all sides of the fillets are gently coated. Set aside for 10 minutes.

Meanwhile, place the potato and eggplant strips in two separate bowls and sprinkle each with another ½ teaspoon of the turmeric and a pinch of salt, rubbing them in to ensure all pieces are well coated.

Place a wide frying pan (skillet) over a medium heat and pour in 2 tablespoons of the oil. When the oil is hot, carefully place the salmon fillets, skin-side down, into the pan. Cook for 2 minutes, then turn and cook for another 2 minutes on the other side until very lightly browned. Gently remove from the pan and place back on the plate.

In the same frying pan, cook the potato strips for about 6 minutes, allowing them to brown slightly too. Remove with a slotted spoon and place back in the bowl.

Repeat with the eggplant strips, cooking for about 4 minutes. Remove with a slotted spoon and place back in the bowl.

Add the remaining 1 tablespoon of oil to the pan and, when hot, add the cumin seeds and bay leaf. Cook for 1 minute, then stir in the onion and sugar. Sauté until the onion is translucent, then add the ginger, chilli and tomatoes along with the remaining ½ teaspoon of turmeric and the ground cumin. Stir well and cook for a further 2 minutes, taking care not to burn the thick mixture. Reduce the heat if it is catching.

Add 250ml (1 cup) water and bring to a gentle simmer. If the heat was reduced previously, increase it slightly now. Carefully add the potato strips and cook for about 5 minutes, then add the eggplant strips and cook for a further 4 minutes. Gently stir. When the gravy starts to simmer again, make 4 empty areas in the pan and place the salmon fillets, skin-side down, in the gaps. Cook for 3–4 minutes.

Taste and check the salt and add more if needed, stir gently, then remove from the heat. Sprinkle with coriander leaves and cover until ready to serve.

Serve with steamed rice and a generous dash of lemon juice.

Bengali Mashed Potato

ALOO SHEDO

serves
2

A spiced-up version of the humble mashed potato, this is the ultimate comfort food. When food stocks are running low at home, or you're feeling lazy, or you've had a few days on the go of indulging in rich food, or you're simply feeling slightly under the weather, this dish, served alongside boiled rice and a light dal, is the perfect solution. We often have this at home, as it's quick and easy to make from the most basic ingredients – ones that are nearly always in the cupboard. When I lived in Kolkata, after a few nights of eating out and entertaining, this would be a meal that we would look forward to.

2 potatoes, peeled and cut into quarters

1 small red onion, finely chopped

1 green chilli, finely chopped

1 handful of coriander (cilantro) leaves, finely chopped

1 teaspoon mustard oil or olive oil

salt, to taste

Place the potatoes in a medium saucepan and cover with boiling water. Bring back to the boil and cook for a further 6–8 minutes until the potatoes are tender to the point of a knife. Drain well.

Put the drained potatoes into a mixing bowl and mash until very smooth with a masher or fork. Add all the remaining ingredients and mix well. Divide the mixture into 8 parts. Roll each part into a ball in the palm of your hand and place on a serving plate.

Serve warm with hot rice and a light dal.

Baked Mustard Salmon Fillets

SHORSHEY MAACH

Traditionally, as with many Bengali fish dishes, once the fish pieces have been cleaned and scaled, they are coated with turmeric and salt and then fried, before the preparation of the actual dish commences. Now, with ovens and grills more readily available in India, people are always on the lookout for how to make dishes healthier without compromising on the taste. We make this dish as an oven bake with all the same ingredients, but it's a lot easier and healthier, as there is no frying involved.

4 salmon fillets, skin on, descaled and boneless

boiled rice, to serve

For the spice paste

2 tablespoons rapeseed (canola) oil or mustard oil

2 teaspoons Greek-style yoghurt

2 teaspoons English mustard powder

1 teaspoon wholegrain mustard

½ teaspoon ground turmeric

½ teaspoon white poppy seeds

1 green chilli, finely chopped

1 tomato, coarsely grated

½ teaspoon salt

Preheat the oven to 180°C (350°F/ gas 4).

Place all the spice paste ingredients in a bowl and mix well into a thick paste.

Line a shallow baking tray with foil and place the salmon fillets on it. Cover the fillets with the spice paste and rub it in well, using your hands to ensure all sides of the fillets are coated. Arrange the fillets skin-side down and bake for 12–15 minutes until cooked through (the fish should easily flake).

Immediately remove from the oven and serve with boiled rice.

Poppy Seed Fritters

POSTOR BORA

serves
4

Posto is a by-product of white poppy seeds and is loved by Bengalis. In fact, the use of white poppy seeds is almost a Bengali obsession. Cooked in many different dishes, it's a versatile ingredient that brings a nutty flavour. Historically, poppy cultivation was a big industry in North India, as part of the terrible opium trade formerly run by the British East India Company. The discovery that the by-product of the trade created tasty dishes that could nourish the workers in their poverty is a typical lesson in Indian frugality and invention.

200 g (1¼ cups) white poppy seeds

150 ml (scant ⅔ cup) lukewarm water, or as needed

1 tablespoon gram flour (besan)

1 green chilli, finely chopped

½ white onion, very finely chopped

½ teaspoon ground turmeric

1 teaspoon salt, or to taste

½ tablespoon rapeseed (canola) oil, plus 1 tablespoon for cooking

Grind the poppy seeds in a coffee or spice grinder for 2 minutes, intermittently turning the seeds with a spoon to ensure they are being evenly ground. You are looking for a semi-coarse and crumbly texture. Empty the ground seeds into a mixing bowl and stir in the water to a thick paste consistency (each poppy seed brand absorbs water differently, so some may need more or less water to obtain the right consistency). Leave to rest for 15 minutes.

Once rested, add the remaining ingredients and stir well to a fairly stiff mixture. Divide the mixture into 12–15 portions and form each portion into a patty, 6 cm (2¼ in) in diameter and 1 cm (½ in) thick.

Heat ½ tablespoon of the cooking oil in a shallow frying pan (skillet) over a medium heat. When hot, take a few fritters and place them in the pan. Make sure not to add too many in one go, otherwise they will break. Cook for about 1 minute on each side until the sides become slightly browned. Remove to a serving dish.

Add the remaining oil to cook the next batch of fritters until they are all fried.

Serve as a starter to dinner, or as a main meal with hot rice and dal, and an onion and chilli salad.

Coriander Chicken

DHANEY CHICKEN

serves
4

This is one of my grandmother's specials, served in a generously filled hand-painted clay pot, with some hot *aloo'r porota* on the side and a small dish of her tomato chutney. Many a time, whenever we went to Kolkata on our family holidays, we would ask her to make this meal – we could never have enough of it. The combination of the intense chicken gravy, with the creaminess of the potato *porota* and the tanginess of the chutney is one I can't easily forget. This dish is popular in many parts of India and every family has their own recipe. Getting recipes from my grandparents' generation is always a challenge as the measurements of spices seem to change a little every time, but the outcome is always delicious.

8 skinless, bone-in chicken thighs

juice of ½ lemon

1 bunch of coriander (cilantro), leaves and stems roughly chopped, with a few leaves reserved for garnish

2–3 tablespoons Greek-style yoghurt

4 garlic cloves

2.5 cm (1 in) fresh ginger, grated

2 green chillies, trimmed

1 tablespoon rapeseed (canola) oil

1½ tablespoons ghee

2 bay leaves

1 cinnamon stick

5 cloves

5 black peppercorns

2 teaspoons cumin seeds

1 onion, finely chopped

½ teaspoon sugar

2 teaspoons ground coriander

1 teaspoon ground cumin

salt, to taste

To serve

Aloo'r Porota (page 196) or *Rooti* (page 197)

steamed Basmati rice

Tomato Aar Pruner Chutney (page 211) (optional)

Score each chicken thigh twice diagonally, about 5 mm (¼ in) deep, on both sides. Lay them flat on a tray that can fit into the fridge. Pour over the lemon juice and sprinkle with ½ teaspoon of salt. Set aside.

Blitz the coriander, 2 tablespoons of the yoghurt, the garlic, ginger, chillies, oil and another ½ teaspoon of salt in a food processor to a thick, smooth paste, adding more yoghurt as needed to get it to come together.

Scoop the paste over the chicken pieces and use your hands to ensure each piece is generously coated. Cover and refrigerate for a minimum of 2 hours, or ideally overnight.

When the chicken is marinated and you are ready to cook, bring the chicken back to room temperature for 30 minutes.

Heat a karai or wok that has a lid over a medium heat and add the ghee. Allow to melt, taking care not to burn

it, then add the bay leaves, cinnamon stick, cloves and peppercorns. Cook for 1 minute, then add the cumin seeds. After 30 seconds, add the onions and stir well until they become translucent, then add the sugar and cook until the onions are light brown and caramelised. Carefully add the marinated chicken and cook for about 8 minutes, stirring occasionally, until the sauce begins to bubble. Stir in the ground coriander and cumin, and cook for a further 4 minutes.

Cover the pan and reduce the heat to low. Cook for a further 14 minutes, stirring a few times to ensure nothing sticks to the base of the pan. Remove the lid and season with salt to taste. If there is lots of liquid, increase the heat to high and allow it to evaporate until a thick sauce has formed and coats the chicken.

Finally, sprinkle the reserved coriander leaves over the chicken and cover until ready to serve.

Lamb and Potato Curry

MANGSHOR JHOL

serves
4

5 tablespoons vegetable oil
   or mustard oil

2 bay leaves

5 cm (2 in) cinnamon stick

6 green cardamom pods,
   lightly crushed

4 cloves

1 star anise

3 white onions, finely sliced

1 teaspoon brown sugar

2 potatoes, peeled and cut
   into quarters

1 teaspoon ground turmeric

200 g (7 oz) tinned chopped tomatoes

2 cm (¾ in) piece of fresh ginger,
   grated

2 large garlic cloves, grated

1 teaspoon ground coriander

1 teaspoon ground cumin

½ teaspoon red chilli powder

500 g (1 lb 2 oz) lamb leg, deboned,
   chopped into 3 cm (1 in) pieces

1½ teaspoons salt

1 teaspoon Bengali Garam Masala (see
   page 218)

1 handful of chopped coriander
   (cilantro)

Tender lamb pieces with soft potatoes cooked in a light, warming gravy, this timeless dish makes a delicious meal served with steaming white rice. Often cooked in pressure cookers to speed up the cooking process, the distinct aroma of this dish escaping kitchen windows and the whistles of the pressure cookers in Kolkata would give away exactly what was cooking in that household. Goat meat is usually used, so it is often referred to as *patha'r mangsho*. The sheer anticipation of my mother's *mangshor jhol* being cooked for dinner filled us with joy as children. The lamb would be cooked in a big pot, which would be laid in the middle of the table for everyone to serve themselves. We would relish every mouthful of the meltingly soft lamb.

Heat 4 tablespoons of the oil in a karai or wok over a medium heat. When hot, add the whole spices and cook until the aromas release. Add the onions, stir well, then add the sugar. Reduce the heat very slightly and cover for 5 minutes, allowing the onions to turn light brown. Stir intermittently.

Meanwhile, place the potatoes in a bowl, sprinkle with ¼ teaspoon of the ground turmeric and turn to coat.

Heat the remaining tablespoon of oil in a small frying pan (skillet) over a medium heat. When hot, add the potatoes and cook on each side for about 2 minutes to lightly brown all over. Remove from the heat and set aside.

Use a hand blender or small food processor to blend the tomatoes to a thick, semi-coarse purée. Set aside.

By this point, the onions should be lightly browned and the oils released. Add the grated ginger to the pan, stir

and cook for 1 minute. Stir in the grated garlic and cook for 2 minutes, then add the blended tomatoes. Add the remaining ¾ teaspoon of ground turmeric along with the ground coriander, cumin and chilli powder. Mix well and cook for a further 5 minutes over a medium–high heat.

Add the lamb and salt to the pan and mix well. Pour in 300 ml (1¼ cups) warm water, stir well, then cover the pan, reduce the heat and cook for 15 minutes, stirring occasionally.

Add the potatoes and garam masala and mix to ensure the potatoes are well coated with the gravy. Cover again and cook for a further 30 minutes over a medium–low heat, stirring occasionally.

Check that the potatoes are fully cooked by poking a knife into them, then remove from the heat, sprinkle with the chopped coriander and keep covered until ready to serve.

Bengali Chicken and Potato Curry

MURGEER JHOL

This dish of chicken pieces cooked in a lightly seasoned gravy with soft creamy potatoes is popular on the dinner table in many households. Adding potatoes to a dish is a particularly Bengali thing. Serve with freshly boiled rice or *rooti*, finely chopped raw onions, lime slices and green chillies.

8 skinless, bone-in chicken drumsticks
    or thigh pieces

2 white potatoes, peeled
    and quartered

1½ teaspoons ground turmeric

3 tablespoons mustard oil or rapeseed
    (canola) oil

2 bay leaves

1 cinnamon stick

1 teaspoon black peppercorns

3 green cardamom pods,
    lightly crushed

2 dried red chillies

4 Bombay/white onions, finely sliced

1 teaspoon sugar

2 tomatoes, roughly chopped

5 garlic cloves, finely grated
    (or 2 teaspoons garlic paste)

2.5 cm (1 in) piece of fresh ginger,
    grated (or 1½ teaspoons ginger
    paste)

½ teaspoon chilli powder

1 teaspoon ground coriander

1 teaspoon ground cumin

400 ml (scant 1⅔ cups) water

1½ teaspoons Bengali Garam Masala
    (see page 218)

1 teaspoon salt, or to taste

Score the chicken pieces 3–4 times on each side and set aside.

In a mixing bowl, combine the potatoes with ½ teaspoon of the turmeric and ½ teaspoon of salt. Mix well to ensure the potatoes are thoroughly coated.

Heat 1 tablespoon of the oil in a large heavy-based pan over a medium heat. When hot, add the potatoes and cook for about 2 minutes on each side to lightly brown all over. Remove to a bowl and set aside.

Add the remaining 2 tablespoons of oil to the same pan, then add the bay leaves, cinnamon stick, peppercorns, cardamom pods and dried chilli. Cook until their aromas release, then add the onions, separating the strands by hand as you add them. Add the sugar and caramelise for 2 minutes until the onions are translucent and beginning to turn light brown.

Add the tomatoes, garlic and ginger, and cook for 3 minutes. Add the chicken pieces and sprinkle in the chilli powder, ground coriander and cumin, and the remaining 1 teaspoon of turmeric. Stir gently but thoroughly, ensuring every ingredient is mixed in well. Cook for 5 minutes, then add the potatoes and measured water. Bring to a simmer, then stir in the garam masala and salt, adjusting to taste. Reduce the heat to low, cover and cook for a further 20 minutes.

Remove the lid and check that the chicken is cooked through, then remove from the heat and keep covered until ready to serve.

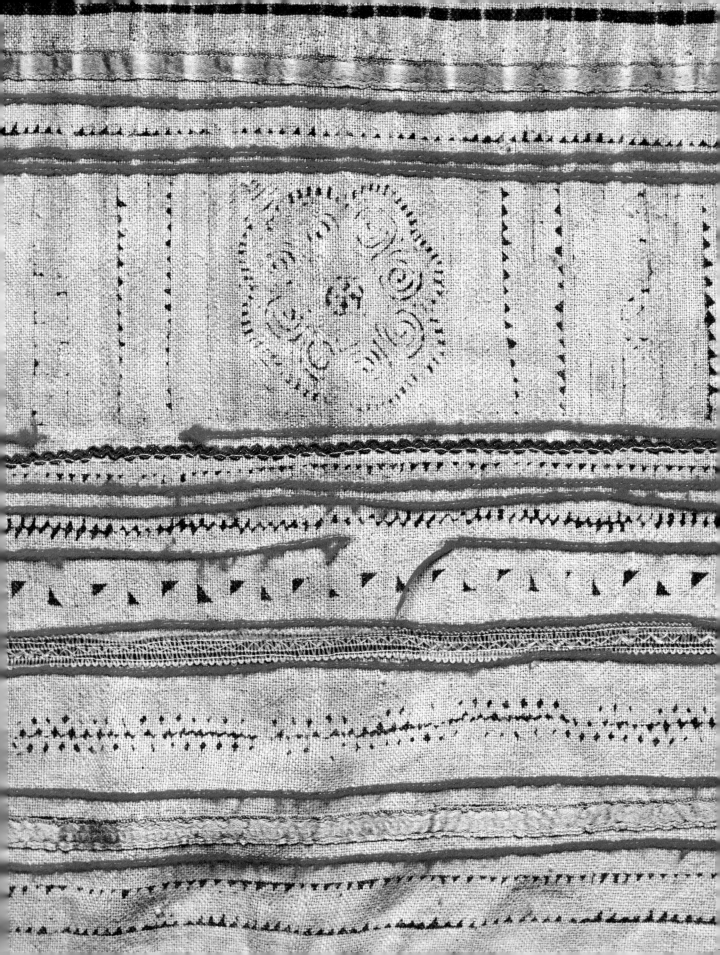

FAMILY FEASTS & FESTIVE MEALS

Evening gatherings are common over the weekend, and families and friends will meet either out at restaurants or in the home. Sundays are a day of feasting, and preparations will start in the morning for the elaborate meals served for breakfast and lunch. I always found the sense of community in Kolkata to be very strong. The need to help and be a part of other people's lives is alive and the one thing that brings everyone together (apart from politics!) is food. The spread of options at these gatherings is often vast, with tables crammed from one side to the other with carefully prepared dishes featuring the catch of the day at the fish markets and fresh *sabji* (vegetables) from the *sabjiwala*. Guests often sit on at the table for hours after finishing their meal, simply talking and laughing. It's such a warm and hospitable atmosphere.

Pretty much all year round, there will some kind of festivity to celebrate in the form of a *puja* (prayers and chanting to a deity, followed by the eating of *prasad*, which is food that has been offered to the god and then to the devotees). These are occasions to dress up and gather with friends and family and there is a beautiful feeling of devotion, with everyone channelling their energy to the same focal point for that day. Surrounded by fresh yellow marigolds, white jasmine flowers, colourful fruit and the fragrance of incense sticks, preparations for *puja* are always joyous moments. After the *puja*, taking *prasad* and eating together is just as important. *Kitchuri* (page 138) and *Labra* (page 140) is a typical meal, with no onion or garlic. In this chapter, I've given you the recipe for *Kitchuri* that we most commonly have at *pujas* – it's also the only comfort food that will do on a cold, wet day, for making everyone in the family feel better.

No wedding is complete without a feast on offer and Bengali weddings definitely don't fall short in this respect. Never a small affair, often hundreds of guests are invited and they will all look forward to devouring a gastronomic extravaganza, often commenting on the size of the shrimp (prawns) served or the number of dishes that were available. For my own wedding in Kolkata, we had different stands offering a variety of styles of food (a tandoor stall, a street-food stall, a fish counter and many more). Wedding food is often very rich, with lots of spices, and I have given you a few of the most popular wedding dishes in this chapter, such as *Kosha Mangso* (page 134) and *Chingri Macher Malaikari* (page 137). They are ideal for any special dinner.

Rich and Thick Lamb Curry

KOSHA MANGSHO

serves
4

750 g (1 lb 10 oz) lamb leg, deboned, cut into 3 cm (1 in) cubes

3 tablespoons mustard oil or rapeseed (canola) oil

1 bay leaf

5 green cardamom pods, lightly crushed

1 black cardamom pod, lightly crushed

5 cloves

1 cinnamon stick

2 dried red chillies

1 whole mace

2 onions, finely chopped

½ teaspoon sugar

1 cm (½ in) piece of fresh ginger, grated

1 garlic clove, grated

250 g (9 oz) chopped tomatoes, mashed into a chunky, thick paste

1 teaspoon ground cumin

1 teaspoon ground coriander

½ teaspoon ground turmeric

½ teaspoon chilli powder

1½ teaspoons salt

1 teaspoon Bengali Garam Masala (see page 218)

1 teaspoon ghee

For the marinade

1 onion, roughly chopped

1 cm (½ in) piece of fresh ginger, peeled

1 garlic clove, peeled

3 tablespoons Greek-style yoghurt

1 tablespoon mustard oil or rapeseed (canola) oil

1 teaspoon salt

½ teaspoon sugar

1 teaspoon ground turmeric

1 teaspoon Bengali Garam Masala (page 218)

Every trip to Kolkata should include a visit to Golbari in Shyam Bazar, an establishment famous for its *kosha mangsho*. The lamb pieces are cooked with spices over a long period of time, making the gravy thick and intensely rich and delicious. Everyone who makes *kosha mangsho* aspires to achieve this flavour, as it's difficult to forget once you've tried it. The dish is a firm favourite served up at most weddings and family gatherings. Traditionally, the wedding meal is served on a banana leaf. Rows and rows of banana leaves will be laid out on long tables and servers come round with silver dishes to serve the guests. Several sittings will take place in the evening to accommodate everyone. There will be a pinch of salt (as Benaglis love to add salt to their meal when eating), chillies and lemon or lime. It's a clever novelty: cheap, because of the vast numbers of banana trees in India; eco-friendly; and easy to dispose of with very little to wash up (a boon as we have such large numbers at weddings).

Blitz the onion, ginger and garlic for the marinade in a blender until coarsely chopped. Transfer to a large bowl, add the remaining marinade ingredients and combine. Add the lamb cubes and mix really well, ensuring all the pieces are well coated in the marinade. Cover and place in the refrigerator to marinate for at least 6 hours (overnight is ideal).

Heat the oil in a heavy-based pan over a medium heat. Add the bay leaf, cardamom pods, cloves, cinnamon stick, dried chillies and the mace, stir gently and let the aromas release. After 1 minute, stir in the onions and sugar. Cover the pan and cook until the onions lightly brown, stirring occasionally. Add the ginger and stir for 1 minute, then add the garlic and cook for a further minute. Add the tomatoes, increase the heat to medium–high and bring to a simmer.

Cook for 2 minutes, then add the marinated lamb and mix well. Sprinkle in the the cumin, coriander, turmeric, chilli powder and salt, stir well and cook over a high heat for 3 minutes, stirring occasionally to stop it sticking to the bottom of the pan. Reduce the heat to low, cover and cook for 30 minutes, letting the gravy gently simmer. Stir every 10 minutes.

Remove the lid, sprinkle the garam masala around the dish and stir well. Re-cover and cook for a further 15 minutes.

Remove the lid and increase the heat to high. Cook until the remaining gravy condenses and the oil starts to release, then add the ghee and stir. Cook for a final 5 minutes, stirring constantly.

Remove from the heat and cover until ready to serve. Serve with rice.

Jumbo Shrimp in a Thick Coconut Gravy

CHINGRI MACHER MALAIKARI

serves
5

The ultimate dish on any Bengali menu, this is usually made for special occasions, such as weddings and dinner feasts. It is a delicate dish that highlights the flavour of the fresh shrimp cooked in a mild coconut gravy. The size of the shrimp is often the topic of conversation at the table. In Kolkata, going early in the morning to the fish market and haggling with the fish seller is all part of the fun. This can be made with all sizes of shrimp, but for entertaining I would use jumbo shrimp (medium/large prawns).

1 kg (2 lb 4 oz) jumbo shrimp (medium/large prawns), deveined and heads removed

1 teaspoon ground turmeric

2 teaspoons salt

2 tablespoons rapeseed (canola) oil

2 teaspoons ghee

2 bay leaves

1 cinnamon stick

3 green cardamom pods

4 cloves

2 onions, blitzed in a blender to a semi-coarse paste

1 teaspoon sugar

2 cm (¾ in) piece of fresh ginger, grated

2 tablespoons Greek-style yoghurt

400 g (14 oz) tinned coconut milk (use one with a high coconut content, above 75%), well shaken

1 tablespoon coconut cream

1 teaspoon Bengali Garam Masala (see page 218)

Combine the shrimp, turmeric and 1 teaspoon of the salt in a bowl and mix well to coat. Leave to marinate for 20 minutes.

Heat 1 tablespoon of the oil in a heavy-based sauté pan over a medium heat. When hot, gently add the shrimp and sauté for 2 minutes until they change colour slightly, but are not fully cooked through. Immediately remove to a bowl and set aside.

Heat the remaining tablespoon of oil along with 1 teaspoon of the ghee in the same pan over a medium heat. Add the bay leaves, cinnamon stick, cardamom and cloves. Cook until the aromas release, then add the onion paste and cook for about 2 minutes, stirring continuously. Mix in the remaining 1 teaspoon of salt along with the sugar, then add the ginger and cook for 1 minute. Stir through the yoghurt and cook for another minute. Add the coconut milk and coconut cream, stirring well to ensure there are no lumps. Check the consistency: if you prefer a thinner sauce, add 4 tablespoons of water (generally the coconut sauce is delicately flavoured, but quite thick). When the sauce begins to simmer, reduce the heat very slightly and add the shrimp. Stir well and cook for 4–5 minutes until the shrimp are fully cooked through.

Finally, sprinkle in the garam masala and add the remaining teaspoon of ghee to the middle of the pan (do not stir). Remove from the heat, cover the pan and leave to rest for 5 minutes before serving. Just before serving, gently mix in the garam masala and melted ghee. Serve with steamed Basmati rice.

Rice and Daal

KITCHURI

serves
5

Kitchuri (sometimes called *khichdi* in some parts of India) is a traditional Ayurvedic dish made of rice and lentils, known for its detoxifying effects on the body, and the inspiration for the Anglo-Indian dish kedgeree. It's a winter one-pot meal made with seasonal vegetables. For me, it holds vivid, fond memories of monsoons and the festive season in Kolkata. Traditionally cooked with one type of lentil, this savoury porridge has a special place in most Bengalis' hearts.

190 g (1 cup) yellow split lentils
    (moong dal)

125 g (⅔ cup) Basmati rice
    (or *gobindo bhog* rice)

3 tablespoons rapeseed (canola) oil

2 white potatoes, peeled and cut into
    quarters

1½ teaspoons ground turmeric

150 g (5 oz) cauliflower, cut into
    small florets

1½ tablespoons ghee

2 teaspoons cumin seeds

2 bay leaves

1 cinnamon stick

3 green cardamom pods

4 cloves

5 cm (2 in) piece of fresh ginger,
    grated

1 dried red chilli

1 tomato, roughly chopped

1 teaspoon sugar

1 teaspoon Bengali Garam Masala (see
    page 218)

½ teaspoon asafoetida

1.5 litres (6 cups) freshly boiled water

50 g (⅓ cup) frozen peas

salt, to taste

To serve

poppadoms

Labra (see page 140)

Aachar (store-bought mango pickle or
    eggplant pickle on page 216)

Heat a medium frying pan (skillet) over a medium heat, add the yellow split lentils and dry-roast for 3–4 minutes, taking care not to burn them. Transfer to a bowl to cool.

Place the rice in a bowl and wash a few times until the water runs clear, then drain and set aside.

In a karai or wok, heat 2 tablespoons of the oil over a medium heat, add the potatoes and ½ teaspoon of the turmeric and ½ teaspoon of salt. Stir well and fry for about 4 minutes until they begin to go slightly brown. Remove with a slotted spoon and set aside.

To the remaining oil in the pan, add the cauliflower florets, along with another ¼ teaspoon of the turmeric and ½ teaspoon of salt. Cook for 5 minutes until they turn light brown. Remove with a slotted spoon and set aside with the potatoes.

Add the remaining 1 tablespoon of the oil and 1 tablespoon of the ghee to a heavy-based pan with a lid, set over a medium heat. Add the cumin seeds, bay leaves, cinnamon stick, cardamom pods and cloves. Cook until the aromas release, then add the ginger, dried chilli and tomatoes. Cook, stirring continuously, for 2 minutes. Add the dry-roasted lentils and the washed rice and cook, stirring, for about 6 minutes. Add the remaining ¾ teaspoon of turmeric along with the sugar, garam masala and asafoetida, and cook for a further 3 minutes.

Add the freshly boiled water, stir well and bring to a gentle simmer, then reduce the heat and cover. Cook for 12 minutes.

Remove the lid and stir once, ensuring nothing is sticking to the base of the pan and that there is still plenty of water in the dish. Add the potatoes and cauliflower, and season with salt, to taste. Cover again and cook over a low heat for a further 10 minutes.

Remove the lid and check that the potatoes are cooked through, then add the frozen peas and cover again for a further 4 minutes.

Finally, drizzle in the remaining ½ tablespoon of ghee, and keep covered until ready to serve.

Serve with poppadoms, *Labra* (vegetable mishmash) and an *Aachar* (pickle) of choice.

Bengali Vegetable Mishmash

LABRA

serves 4

Cooked with the Bengali five spice (paanch phoron), this vegetable dish is lightly mashed and semi-dry in consistency. It goes perfectly with *Kitchuri* (page 128) and is often served as *prasad* after *pujas* (see page 142), along with *Aloo Bhaja* (page 52), *Tomato Aar Pruner Chutney* (page 211), *Payesh* (page 175) and a *mishti* (sweet). It's a *puja* delight! *Labra* is also made at home as part of a weekday dinner. It is very economical as you can also add the stalks of the veg, using up all parts. When my mother cooks this, she drizzles in a little bit of mustard oil right at the end, giving it a wonderful aroma.

3 tablespoons mustard oil or rapeseed (canola) oil

1 small eggplant (aubergine), cut into 1.5 cm (½ in) cubes

1 tablespoon ghee

2 dried red chillies

2 teaspoons Bengali Paanch Phoron (page 218)

2 bay leaves

50 g (2 oz) potatoes, peeled and cut into 1.5 cm (½ in) cubes

50 g (2 oz) sweet potatoes, peeled and cut into 1.5 cm (½ in) cubes

60 g (2¼ oz) pumpkin, cut into 1.5 cm (½ in) cubes

50g (2 oz) yard-long beans (*borboti*)

50 g (2 oz) zucchini (courgette), cut into 1.5 cm (½ in) discs, then each disc quartered

60 g (2¼ oz) cauliflower, broken into tiny florets

1 teaspoon grated fresh ginger

1 teaspoon sugar

1 teaspoon salt

1 teaspoon ground turmeric

2.5 cm (1 in) piece of fresh ginger, cut into very fine strips

½ teaspoon Jeera Bhaja Masala (page 218)

1 teaspoon mustard oil, for drizzling

Heat 2 tablespoons of the oil in a wok or kadai over a medium heat. Add the eggplant and cook for 3 minutes, carefully turning a little until browned. Remove to drain on a plate lined with kitchen paper.

Add the remaining tablespoon of oil and the ghee to the same pan. When the ghee has melted, add the dried chillies, paanch phoron and the bay leaves, and allow the whole spices to crackle and the aromas to release. Add the potatoes and sweet potatoes, stir well and cook for 4 minutes. Add the pumpkin, beans, zucchini and cauliflower, then add the grated ginger and mix well. Cook for 5 minutes, then add the sugar, salt and ground turmeric. Stir thoroughly. Reduce the heat, cover and cook for a further 10 minutes.

By now, the water from the vegetables should have released. Add the ginger strips and fold in, then add the fried eggplant. Increase the heat to medium and cook for about 7 minutes to allow the excess water to evaporate. Sprinkle over the bhaja masala and the teaspoon of mustard oil and cover until ready to serve.

Fish Steaks in Yoghurt

DOI MAACH

Using fleshy fish, this rich dish is cooked with yoghurt, which brings a tangy flavour. In Kolkata it is made with *hilsa*, but I am using salmon steaks. Popular on occasions for feasting, I have memories of being served this dish at weddings on *shal patta* leaves.

1 Bombay/white onion, roughly chopped

2.5 cm (1 in) piece of fresh ginger, peeled

5 garlic cloves, peeled

4 tablespoons full-fat plain yoghurt

4 skin-on, bone-in salmon steaks, approx 1.5 cm (⅔ in) thick

1½ teaspoons ground turmeric

3 tablespoons mustard oil or rapeseed (canola) oil

2 bay leaves

4 green cardamom pods

1 cinnamon stick

5 cloves

1 dried red chilli

1 teaspoon cumin seeds

1½ teaspoons sugar

½ teaspoon chilli powder

1 teaspoon ground cumin

1 teaspoon Bengali Garam Masala (see page 218)

1 tablespoon finely chopped coriander (cilantro)

salt, to taste

Combine the onion, ginger, garlic, 2 tablespoons of the yoghurt and 2 tablespoons of water in a blender and blitz to a semi-smooth paste (if the yoghurt is very thick, you may need to add another teaspoon of water). Set aside.

Place the salmon steaks on a plate, sprinkle over ½ teaspoon of the turmeric and ½ teaspoon of salt, and gently rub in to coat the fish evenly.

Heat 2 tablespoons of the oil in a medium sauté pan that has a lid over a medium heat. When hot, gently lower the salmon steaks into the oil and cook for 2 minutes on each side until lightly browned. Remove to a plate and set aside.

Add the remaining tablespoon of oil to the same pan and heat. Add the bay leaves, cardamom pods, cinnamon stick, cloves and the dried chilli. Cook until the aromas release, then reduce the heat, add the cumin seeds and cook for 1 minute. Spoon in the onion paste (it will sizzle), then add the sugar and stir for 3 minutes. When the oil begins to release from the sauce, add the chilli powder, ground cumin, the remaining 1 teaspoon of turmeric and the garam masala and mix well.

In a small bowl, combine the remaining 2 tablespoons of yoghurt with 4 tablespoons of water and mix to a thin paste. Add this mixture to the pan, increase the heat to medium and bring to a simmer. Season with salt to taste. Add the salmon steaks to the pan, spooning some of the gravy over the fish, then reduce the heat, cover and cook for 6 minutes. Remove the lid and sprinkle over the coriander, then remove from the heat and cover until ready to serve.

Festivals

As a city that homes many different religions, Kolkata boasts a huge number of festivals and fairs throughout the year. Naturally, food plays a huge part in the festivities.

The most important of these festivals is *Durga Puja*, a five-day carnival of worship for the goddess Durga and the victory of good over evil, which usually takes place in October. Schools and offices are closed for all five days and it's a time when family and friends get together to pray, rejoice, dance and feast. New clothes are worn and people are full of happiness. It's a long holiday and eagerly anticipated every year. *Durga Puja* is celebrated all over the city and many streets are closed so that the *pandals* (decorated temple scaffolds) can be built in the roads or parks. Local clubs and committees spend months organising the *puja*. Each *pandal* is illuminated and features a clay goddess who is beautifully adorned. The clay idols are handcrafted in Kumartuli Potter Town in North Kolkata and take months to complete.

During this time, feasts are made, both at home and also at the *pujas*. At the *pandals*, a variety of vegetarian dishes are cooked and first offered to the idols, after which devotees are offered the food to consume (this is called *prasad*). Dishes such as *kitchuri* (page 138),

luchi (page 192) and *mishti* (page 172) are just some of the most popular. The streets are bustling, loud music plays from speakers in the streets, there is dancing, street food vendors have queues of people at their stalls, businesses are booming and the whole vibe of the city is one of celebration and joy!

Doljatra , also known as *Dolyatra*, is another very popular festival in West Bengal. Celebrated on the same day as *Holi*, the last full moon in the Hindu calendar, this festival is dedicated to Lord Krishna and Radha. *Doljatra* translates to 'swing procession', which refers to the platforms that bear the idols of Krishna and Radha that are swung around in the air. Like *Holi*, it is also sometimes called the 'festival of colour'. People throw coloured powders called *abir* at each other and liquid colours are sprayed all around. Many milk products are made to consume during this time and sweet rice (*mishti pilau*, page 201) is also enjoyed.

Kali Puja usually follows on a few weeks after *Durga Puja*. This *puja* is performed at night and uses the hibiscus flower as an offering. Large clay idols symbolising the destruction of evil are worshipped. Whereas vegetarian or *satvic* dishes are made for other religious festivals, meat is offered to the goddess

during this celebration and is eaten by the worshippers, too. *Satvic* dishes contain no onion or garlic and are eaten for a well-balanced, healthy body and a calm mind (*satvic* means 'pure essence' in Sanskrit).

Saraswati Puja, also known as *Vasant Pachami*, is held on the first day of spring and celebrates the goddess of knowledge and wisdom, Saraswati. Offerings of fruits, sweets and nuts are laid in front of the embellished idol, while a priest says the prayers. Children wear yellow and seek blessing from the goddess before having *prasad*, which is usually *kitchuri* (page 138).

The Kolkata Book Fair is held at the end of January. This 12-day fair is one of the largest in Kolkata and ardent book lovers look forward to this time to get their hands on rare treats.

The dance and music scene play a big part in Bengalis' lives. Singing and dancing classes are encouraged from a young age and there is great popular appreciation of such arts. The Dover Lane Music Festival started off as a small gathering of music lovers, each performing their own music. Over the years, as more people took interest and came to watch it, the festival grew. Now, it is one of the most reputable music festivals in India. Artists from far and wide perform and thousands come to watch.

Banana-Leaf Steamed Mustard Fish

MAACHER PATHURI

serves 4

I once saw this made on a visit to an outlying *gram* (village), where the grandmother of the household cooked it on an open fire outside her mud hut with freshly caught white fish. Traditionally, *hilsa/ilish* (a type of herring) is used to make this dish, but I use cod. The marinade of mustard seeds ground to a paste in a *sil nora* (a large pestle and mortar) was just so fresh and aromatic. In this recipe, I steam the fish, but it can also be fried with the leaves too with minimal oil.

Banana leaves have so many uses in India – hygienic, eco-friendly and economical, they are used as serving plates as well as for wrapping and steaming dishes, as here. They can be sourced in most Asian grocery stores that sell fresh produce and they do bring a certain earthiness to the dish. If you can't find banana leaves, you can of course use sheets of greaseproof paper instead.

---

4 skinless and boneless cod fillets, ideally 1 cm (½ in) thick

2 tablespoons mustard oil or rapeseed (canola) oil

2 tablespoons wholegrain mustard

2 teaspoons English mustard

1 green chilli, roughly chopped

2 teaspoons poppy seeds

1 teaspoon desiccated (dried unsweetened shredded) coconut

1 teaspoon salt, or to taste

4 sheets of fresh banana leaves

boiled rice, to serve

Trim each cod fillet to make the pieces unifrom in size (this is optional). Place on a plate and pat dry of any excess moisture. Set aside.

In a blender, combine the oil, both mustards, chilli, poppy seeds, coconut and salt, and blitz to a thick paste. Be sure not to add any water – if the paste is too thick, add another tablespoon of oil.

Spoon the paste over the cod fillets and coat all sides of the fish well. Take a banana leaf and place one cod fillet on the matt side of the leaf. Wrap the leaf around the fillet, cutting away any excess, but ensuring the fillet is fully wrapped. Tie a length of kitchen string around the leaf to hold it in place. Repeat with the remaining banana leaves and fillets.

Set a steamer basket over a pan of boiling water (or use a steamer pan) and set over a low–medium heat. Place the parcels into the steamer and cover with the lid. Steam for 10 minutes. After this time the fish should be cooked through, but you may want to open one parcel to check.

Place the parcels on a serving plate, keeping the leaves on to retain the moisture. Serve with plain white rice and unwrap at the table.

Kebabs with Saffron Rice

CHELO KEBAB

Chelo kebab is the national dish of Iran and simply translates to 'rice and kebab'. The go-to place in Kolkata to indulge in this is Peter Cat. Famous for its ambience and *chelo kebabs*, it is a must on any visit to Kolkata. Nitin Kothari opened the restaurant in 1975, inspired by a trip to Tehran and wanting to introduce this dish to the city. It is a substantial meal consisting of saffron rice, mincemeat kebabs, grilled chicken pieces, cubes of butter and a fried egg to top it all off!

Although it is rather time consuming to prepare, it's definitely a 'wow' dish to serve up to guests. You need to cook the dishes in the correct order so that all are ready at nearly the same time. Marinade the meats, soak the rice, cook the meats and, when the meats are nearly cooked, finish cooking the rice. Finally, cook the fried eggs before plating up.

Optional if not using a barbecue

2 pieces of charcoal

1 teaspoon vegetable oil

For the saffron water

a pinch of saffron strands

2 tablespoons water

For the lamb kebabs (8 skewers)

2 white onions, roughly chopped

2 green chillies, roughly chopped

6 garlic cloves, roughly chopped

2.5 cm (1 in) piece of fresh ginger, chopped

100 g (generous 1 cup) fresh breadcrumbs

2 tablespoons rapeseed (canola) oil

3 eggs

2 teaspoons ground cumin

2 teaspoons ground coriander

2 teaspoons sumac

4 tablespoons finely chopped coriander (cilantro)

1½ teaspoons salt

750 g (1 lb 11 oz) minced (ground) lamb (10% fat)

1 tablespoon unsalted butter, melted (optional)

For the chicken and tomato kebabs (9 skewers)

1 kg (2 lb 4 oz) skinless boneless chicken thighs, cut into 2.5 cm (1 in) cubes

3 tablespoons freshly squeezed lime juice

2 green cardamom pods

50 g (⅓ cup) unsalted cashew nuts

3 teaspoons dried fenugreek leaves

1 teaspoon freshly ground black pepper

1 teaspoon anardana powder (pomegranate powder)

1 tablespoon rapeseed (canola) oil

2 tablespoons double (heavy) cream

3 garlic cloves, grated

2 cm (¾ in) piece of fresh ginger, grated

1 teaspoon ground turmeric

1 teaspoon salt

6 green bell peppers (capsicums), cut into 2 cm (¾ in) squares

4 Bombay/white onions, quartered and petals separated

4 tomatoes

For the saffron rice

175 g (scant 1 cup) long-grain Basmati rice

2 tablespoons ghee

¼ teaspoon saffron strands

2 teaspoons salt

4 green cardamom pods, lightly crushed

¼ teaspoon yellow food colouring

For the eggs

1 tablespoon rapeseed (canola) oil

4 eggs

freshly ground black pepper, to taste

To serve

8 x 1 cm (½ in) cubes of cold butter

Before you prepare either kebab, prepare the saffron water and marinate the meats. Combine the saffron and water in a bowl and set aside to infuse. The meats will need at least 2–3 hours to marinate.

FOR THE LAMB KEBABS

Place the onions, chillies, garlic and ginger in a food processor and blitz until finely chopped. Empty into a large mixing bowl (wash the food processor and dry thoroughly). Add the breadcrumbs to the bowl, along with the oil, eggs, ground spices, coriander, salt, lamb and 2 teaspoons of the infused saffron water. With clean hands, mix the ingredients together thoroughly. Cover with cling film (plastic wrap) and place in the fridge for a minimum of 2 hours.

Meanwhile, heat a barbecue. If you don't have a barbecue, preheat the grill (broiler) to medium and preheat the oven to 180°C (350°F/gas 4).

When the lamb has marinated, divide the meat into 8 equal portions. With wet hands, flatten each portion of the meat evenly along the length of a skewer to about 20 cm (8 in) long and 1 cm (½ in) thick. Once the mince has set on the skewers, use your index finger to gently press along each kebab to give it a ribbed effect. Place on a grilling tray. Barbecue or grill the kebabs for 5 minutes on each side, or until fully cooked.

For a char flavour if you cooked them on the grill, use a fork to gently ease the kebabs off the skewer and place them on a baking sheet. Coat them lightly with melted butter. Form a piece of foil into a cup shape and place it in the middle of the baking sheet among the kebabs. Have another piece of foil, slightly larger

than the tray, ready. With tongs, place a piece of charcoal over a flame to light it, then immediately place the coal in the cupped foil and pour the vegetable oil over the coal. Cover the tray immediately with the extra foil and place in the oven for 10 minutes.

FOR THE CHICKEN AND TOMATO KEBABS

Place the chicken in a large bowl along with the lime juice and 1 teaspoon of salt. Set aside for 30 minutes.

In a spice grinder, grind the cardamom, cashews and fenugreek leaves to a fine powder. Add the powder to the chicken bowl along with the pepper, anardana powder, rapeseed oil, cream, garlic, ginger, turmeric, 1 tablespoon of the saffron water and the salt. Mix well, ensuring the chicken pieces are fully coated with the mixture.

Take a skewer and pierce through a chicken piece followed by a piece of bell pepper and then a piece of onion. Repeat until each kebab is about 25 cm (10 in) long. Make 8 skewers in the same way, taking care not to pack them too tightly. Place on a baking sheet, leaving space between each so that air can circulate.

Pierce the tomatoes through the middle on the final skewer and add to the tray. Cover and place in the fridge for a minimum of 2 hours.

When the chicken has marinated, bring to room temperature for 30 minutes. Ensure the barbecue (or grill and oven) is ready, as above.

Barbecue or grill each kebab for about 17 minutes, rotating the skewers evenly every few minutes until the chicken is fully cooked. The tomatoes will need less time to char on all sides.

For a char flavour if you cooked them on the grill, follow the same method as for the lamb kebabs, above, but keeping them on their skewers.

FOR THE SAFFRON RICE

Wash the rice carefully in a saucepan a few times until the water runs clear. Cover the rice with fresh water and leave to soak for 1 hour. Drain well.

Start cooking the rice only when the meats are nearly cooked. Melt the ghee in a heavy-based pan over a medium heat, then add the rice and saffron and sauté for 3 minutes.

Meanwhile, boil a kettle.

Add 320 ml (1¼ cups) of boiling water to the rice along with the salt and cardamom pods. Cook over a medium heat for 10 minutes. Add the yellow food colouring and stir, then switch off the heat and cover for 10 minutes before serving.

FOR THE EGGS

Heat the oil in a frying pan (skillet) over a medium heat, then crack in the eggs and fry sunny-side-up for about 4 minutes. Remove from the pan and season with black pepper.

TO SERVE

Just as you're ready to serve, cut the cold cubes of butter. Arrange a thick line of rice along the middle of each serving plate. Place 2 lamb kebabs and 2 chicken kebabs on either side of the rice. Take a tomato from the skewer and place on one side of the plate. Place 2 cubes of butter on top of the rice and finally top with the fried egg.

Pictured overleaf

Beef Bhuna

KALO BHUNA

serves
4

1 kg (2 lb 4 oz) beef chuck (7-bone) steak
1 tablespoon mustard oil
2 tablespoons ghee
2 bay leaves
3 Bombay/white onions, finely sliced
1 teaspoon sugar
2 garlic cloves, finely grated
1 green chilli, slit lengthways
4 tablespoons tamarind paste (You can soak a block of tamarind in boiling water for 45 minutes, then push through a fine strainer to obtain the paste. If so, use 2 tablespoons only.)
2 teaspoons Jeera Bhaja Masala (see page 218)

For the marinade

1 teaspoon coriander seeds
1 teaspoon cumin seeds
4 green cardamom pods
1 black cardamom pod
4 red Kashmiri chillies
1 mace
1 teaspoon cloves
1 Bombay/white onion, roughly chopped
6 garlic cloves
2.5 cm (1 in) piece of fresh ginger
2 tablespoons Greek-style yoghurt
2 tablespoons fresh lemon juice
1 teaspoon fennel seeds
1 teaspoon black peppercorns
1 teaspoon ground turmeric
1 tablespoon rapeseed (canola) oil
1 teaspoon salt

To serve

handful of coriander (cilantro), chopped
2.5 cm (1 in) piece of fresh ginger, sliced into thin strips
lemon wedges (optional)
Rooti (page 197) or *Porota* (page 196)

This is a slow-cooked, intensely flavoured dish, popular in the area of Alipore in Kolkata, which you will find served in many restaurants. As beef is not eaten by Hindus (the cow is considered a sacred animal), this is a Muslim dish. It is usually served with *rumali rooti*, which means 'handkerchief roti' because they are so thin and large. The art of making these *rooti* is quite a treat – thrown in the air and stretched to nearly half a metre in diameter, they are an ideal match for this dish. The *porota* (on page 196) pair very well too. Make sure to get steak with the bone in, as it improves the flavour of this dish immensely.

First, make the marinade. Heat a small frying pan (skillet) over a medium heat. Add all the spices and dry-roast for about 4 minutes, shaking the pan frequently to prevent burning. Let the roasted spices cool, then blitz to a fine powder in a spice grinder.

Meanwhile, place the chopped onion, garlic, ginger, yoghurt and lemon juice in a food processor and blitz to a thick paste. Transfer to a mixing bowl and combine with 2 tablespoons of the roasted ground spices, the fennel seeds, peppercorns, turmeric, rapeseed oil and salt.

Cut the beef into 3 cm (1¼ in) cubes with the bone in, add them to the bowl and mix well with a wooden spoon, ensuring the meat is well coated. Marinate in the fridge for 2–3 hours.

When ready to cook, heat a heavy-based pan over a medium heat, then add the mustard oil and ghee. Add the bay leaves and the finely sliced onions and separate the strands with a wooden spoon. Cook for 3 minutes

until translucent, then add the sugar, garlic and green chilli. Stir well and cook for 2 minutes. Add the marinated meat with its marinade, stir well and cook for 5–6 minutes. Bring to a bubble, then stir in the tamarind paste, reduce the heat to low, cover and cook for 40 minutes.

Remove the lid and stir well. If it's really dry, add 200 ml (scant 1 cup) water and bring to a bubble. Add 1 teaspoon of the bhaja moshla and mix again. Cover and cook for another 30 minutes over a low heat.

Remove the lid. If there is a lot of excess liquid, increase the heat and reduce the sauce, or add more water as needed. You want a thick sauce that coats the meat very well. Remove from the heat and stir through the remaining teaspoon of bhaja masala.

Serve hot, garnished with chopped coriander and a few strips of ginger. Lemon wedges can also be served on the side, along with your choice of breads.

Ron's Chicken Biryani

CHICKEN BIRYANI

For the biryani masala

1 tablespoon caraway seeds

8 green cardamom pods

1 black cardamom pod

1 star anise

1 mace

¼ nutmeg

8 cloves

2 teaspoons coriander seeds

2 teaspoons allspice

1 teaspoon fennel seeds

1 teaspoon black peppercorns

For the chicken and gravy

rapeseed (canola) oil, for deep-frying

8 onions: 4 thinly sliced; 4 finely chopped

1 tablespoon sugar

5 garlic cloves, finely grated

3.5 cm (1½ in) fresh ginger, grated

2 teaspoons garam masala

4 tomatoes, blitzed in a food processor

4 bone-in skinless chicken thighs

4 skinless chicken drumsticks

1 teaspoon anardana powder

1 pinch of saffron strands

100 ml (scant ½ cup) full-fat milk

2 tablespoons ghee

2 tablespoons torn coriander (cilantro)

For the rice

400 g (2 cups) premium Basmati rice

2 bay leaves

4 star anise

6 green cardamom pods

6 cloves

4 cinnamon sticks

2 whole nutmeg

4 teaspoons salt

¼ teaspoon yellow food colouring

2 drops of attar (scented oil – optional)

I've grown up eating my dad's biryani and it is essential at our home-celebrated occasions. Biryani is another Persian dish that each city in India has adapted to its own, with slight variations. In Kolkata, it is the addition of potatoes. The biryani masala can be made in small batches and kept for about a month to maintain the strength and aroma of the spices. Serve with a raita or salad.

Wash the rice and leave to soak in fresh water for 2 hours.

Grind the spices for the biryani masala in a spice grinder. Store in a sealed jar.

Heat enough oil for deep-frying in a large saucepan. Deep-fry the thinly sliced onions until golden brown. Remove with a slotted spoon to drain on kitchen paper. Set aside.

In a large heavy-based pot that has a lid, heat 3 tablespoons of oil over a medium–high heat. Add the chopped onions and fry, stirring, for 1 minute, then add the sugar and continue to cook until browned. Cover and cook for a further 5 minutes. Add the garlic and ginger and cook for 3 minutes, then add the garam masala and the blitzed tomatoes, stir through and cook until the oil releases. Score the chicken pieces and add to the pot, then add 1½ tablespoons of the biryani masala mixture along with the anardana powder and cook for 5 minutes. Reduce the heat to low, cover and cook for 30 minutes.

In a small glass, soak the saffron in the milk. Set aside.

Preheat oven to 180°C (350°F/gas 4).

Drain the rice. Bring 2 saucepans of water to the boil, add half of the whole spices to each pan, bring back to the boil and add 2 teaspoons of salt to each. Divide the rice equally between the 2 pans and add the yellow food colouring to one of the pans. Boil for 6 minutes, then drain both separately, reserving the cooking water from the white rice.

Coat the bottom of a large casserole (Dutch oven) with a thin layer of ghee. Add 4 tablespoons of the rice cooking water, a third of the white rice in a thin layer, then a third of the yellow rice, then half of the chicken with the gravy. Next, add another third of the white rice, half of the saffron milk, half of the fried onions and the coriander leaves. Top with another third of the yellow rice, the remaining chicken and gravy and the remaining white rice. Finish with a final layer of the yellow rice, the remaining fried onions, and the remaining saffron milk. Add the attar, if using. Cover the casserole with the lid and tightly seal with foil (or dough to be traditional). Bake in the oven for 30 minutes.

Break the seal and serve immediately.

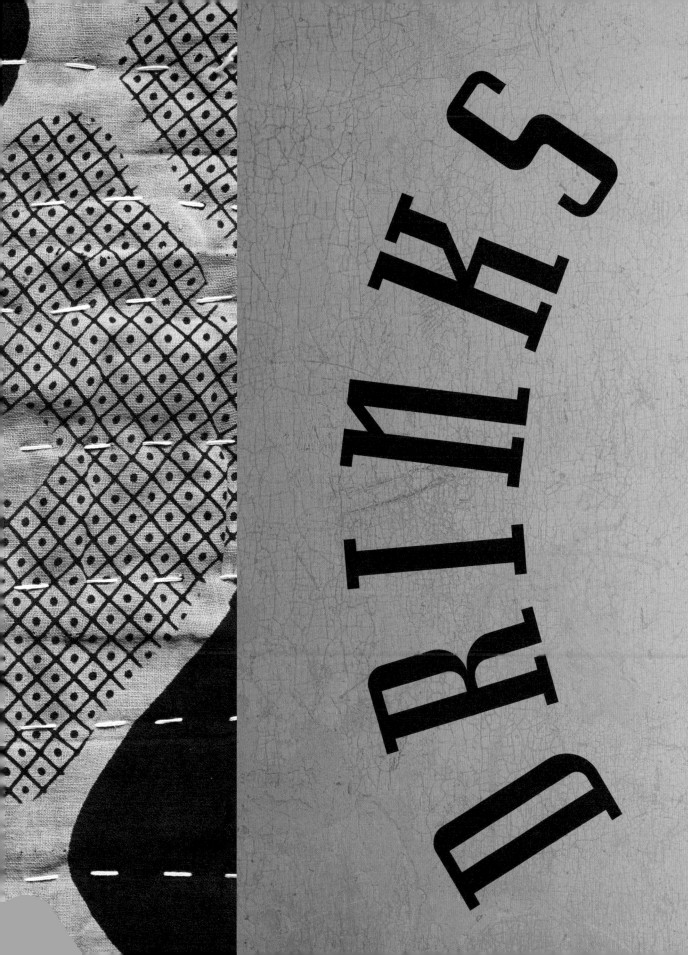

DRINKS

There is such a wide variety of hot and cold drinks available in Kolkata. Many are seasonal, made from the fresh fruits found in and around the city. The juice bars near Decker's (Dacres) Lane are bedecked with colourful fruit hanging from every place possible, and any combination of fruits will be whizzed up in an instant for you to enjoy.

Some drinks with specific health benefits are made to deal with the extreme weather conditions. *Dhaab*, for instance, are young green coconuts that are sliced on the top and served with a straw and are consumed for their cooling benefits. Often, the white sweet flesh is scooped out and eaten, too. These are one of the things I look forward to the most whenever I visit Kolkata. You can see the *dhaab* sellers, who will have climbed many coconut trees early in the morning, then hung the fresh coconuts on either side of their bicycles, stopping from road to road to wait for their customers.

Sugar cane juice (*akher rosh*) is another popular drink, made from sugar canes that are put through a set of cogs that repeatedly extract the sugar cane juice in its raw state. One vendor who stands outside New Market, turning the wheel of his slightly chipped, blue-painted cogs, makes the most frothy *akher rosh*. His is a place I find any excuse to visit whenever I am in the city.

The all-time favourite drink, though, is tea (*cha*) and it will be consumed several times throughout the day. Although coffee shops are very popular places for friends to meet up, tea is inifitely more popular than coffee in the city. Served in small clay pots called *bhaar* and often very small in size, the usual type of *cha* that is readily available on the streets of Kolkata is a sweet, milky, intensely flavoured tea. You will often see a *chawala* walking around with a silver teapot in one hand and a wire basket filled with small glasses or *bhaar* in the other. Many breakfast joints serve tea, too, along with their savoury and sweet specialities.

As India is very well known for its tea estates, there are many tea houses that you can visit that stock the most aromatic tea leaves. Types such as Darjeeling and Makaibari are served in fine china cups in these special tea rooms. The tea is served with no milk, so the real taste of the tea comes through. My favourite is the First Flush brew, which I enjoy in a small, quaint tea room in Dakshinapan called Dolly's – The Tea Shop. You can also buy the tea leaves from here, which make perfect gifts.

The selection of drinks I have given you in this chapter are all easy to make and the ingredients can be sourced and enjoyed in colder countries, too.

Cardamom Tea

ELACHI CHA

serves 2

I love to enjoy a cup of *cha*, served in a little clay *bhar*, while watching the sunset along the Princep *ghat*, or when sitting on a train in a station while tea vendors (*chawala*) jump in and out of each carriage with the glasses stacked high in one hand and a steel kettle in the other, shouting: *chai, chai, garam garam chai* (tea, tea, hot hot tea).

The aroma of this tea is beautiful. Usually it is made from loose black tea leaves that have been brewing for hours and hours. The tea vendors simply top it up with new ingredients, so it's actually very strong. As a result of this, the amount served is quite small and can often be finished within a couple of sips. Of course, when we make it at home, it's not as strong, so serving it in a regular teacup or a glass is completely fine.

500 ml (2 cups) water

2 Yorkshire tea bags and 1 Earl Grey tea bag OR 4 teaspoons loose black tea leaves

3 green cardamom pods, lightly crushed

3 saffron strands

2–3 tablespoons condensed milk (depending on taste)

Place a saucepan over a medium heat and add the water and either the tea bags or tea leaves. After 3 minutes, once the pan has started warming a little, add the cardamom and saffron. Bring to a gentle boil, reducing the heat to low once the tea mixture starts to boil.

Add the condensed milk according to your taste and stir. Increase the heat to medium and bring back to a rolling boil for 2 minutes.

Remove from the heat, allow the bubbles to calm, then place a strainer on each cup and pour the desired amount of tea. Enjoy!

Aromatic Spiced Tea

MASALA CHAI

serves 2

This recipe is a traditional way of making an infused cup of tea. Often called *doodh cha*, this method of making tea can be seen on most streets in Kolkata, with the loose tea leaves continuously bubbling away in a big saucepan. To serve, it is poured from a height into clay vessels or short glasses to create a airy froth on top. Simply delicious.

300 ml (1¼ cups) water

300 ml (1¼ cups) full-fat milk

5 teaspoons loose black tea leaves

1 cinnamon stick

3 green cardamom pods

2 cloves

2 teaspoons brown sugar

Heat the water and the milk in a saucepan over a medium heat for 5 minutes, then add the loose tea leaves, cinnamon stick, cardamom, cloves and sugar. Bring to a simmer, then reduce the heat and gently simmer for a further 5 minutes.

Place a strainer on top of each glass then gently pour the tea from a height into the glass.

Serve immediately and take care as you drink, as it will be very hot.

Savoury Lassi

GHOL

serves
4

Ghol is the Bengali version of the famous *lassi* – a yoghurt drink known for its cooling properties that is enjoyed during the summer months in Kolkata. Summers in Kolkata are very hot, and although we have air conditioners in cars and at home, the general feel is very humid, quite different from other cities, such as Delhi, which have a dry heat. Staying hydrated is very important as you lose lots of water throughout the day. *Ghol* is light and frothy and comes in both sweet and savoury versions. This recipe is for a savoury *ghol* and is very refreshing.

250 g (1 cup) Greek-style yoghurt
150 ml (scant ⅔ cup) cold water
1½ teaspoons black salt (*kala namak*)
2 tablespoons sugar
zest and juice of 1 lime (about 1 teaspoon zest and 2 tablespoons juice)
4 ice cubes

In a blender, combine the yoghurt, water, black salt, sugar and lime juice. Blitz a couple of times until the mixture has blended together and become slightly frothy.

Add an ice cube to each glass and pour over the *ghol*, dividing the froth evenly between them. Sprinkle some lime zest over the froth and serve immediately.

Sparkling Lime Drink

LEBUR JHOL

serves
4

In India, the rooftops of most buildings are accessible, and it is here that people dry their clothes, and dry fruits and preserves. Often, after the afternoon nap, many will go up to the roof (*chaath*) to have their cup of tea. They overlook other buildings and neighbours are often seen having a chat across the voids. From our *chaath*, the summer sunsets were just incredible and during the summer months, when it was too hot to enjoy *cha*, I would make this refreshing drink and enjoy the setting sun.

For this recipe, the *Gondhoraj lebu* lime is traditionally used. It is the most aromatic citrus fruit, hence the name, which translates as 'king of lemon smells'. It doesn't have much juice, but the aroma elevates any dish. Here, I use regular limes as a substitute.

6 tablespoons freshly squeezed lime juice

3 tablespoons sugar

½ teaspoon salt

ice cubes

400 ml (1⅔ cups) sparkling water

½ teaspoon chopped mint leaves

In a jug, combine the lime juice, sugar and salt. Mix well until the sugar and salt have dissolved.

Equally divide the mixture among 4 glasses and add a couple of ice cubes to each glass. Top up with sparkling water and sprinkle each with a little chopped mint. Enjoy.

Mango Drink

AAM PORA SHORBOT

serves 10

A smoky, sweet, sour and refreshing summer drink – so popular in Kolkata. Raw mangoes are a fruit that help the cooling of the body in the hot summer months and are used in many dishes like dals (*tok daal* – sour dal) and dry *torkaris*, too. This drink uses raw mango, but an additional step is to smoke it first. In Kolkata, you will see street vendors placing these small green mangoes on open charcoal fires, releasing a distinct smoky aroma. At home, the mangoes can be smoked directly on an open flame, or if you wish, even on a barbecue, to achieve a more smoky taste.

Green raw mangoes can be found in most Indian grocery stores (don't use any unripe mango from the supermarket), as can black salt (*kala namak*).

3 green raw mangoes

2 tablespoons brown sugar

8 mint leaves

1 teaspoon black salt (*kala namak*)

½ teaspoon Jeera Bhaja Masala (page 218)

ice-cold water and ice cubes, to serve

Wash the mangoes and dry well. Place them directly over a low–medium flame and char all over, carefully turning with tongs after 3–4 minutes on each side. The outside should become charred and they should start to become soft. Once all sides have been charred, carefully remove and place on a plate. Allow to fully cool.

Once cooled, peel the mangoes and spoon and squeeze the pulp into a blender, taking as much pulp off the skin as possible. Add the sugar, mint, black salt and about 125 ml (½ cup) of water. Blend to a semi-thick slush.

Carefully pour the mixture into a glass bottle that can be stored in the fridge. This is the *aam pora* concentrate.

To make the drink, spoon 2 tablespoons of the concentrate into each glass and top up with ice-cold water. Taste and add another tablespoon of concentrate if you'd like a more intense flavour. Add ice cubes and serve. Cheers!

Sweets, *mishti*, are an important part of the culture in West Bengal and a way of life. They are offered for practically any occasion: celebrations, festivities, when guests pop round impromptu or even just when sitting down to a cup of tea. Bengalis don't need a reason or time of day to have *mishti*! On a visit to someone's house, taking sweets as a gift is customary, and you will always be offered sweets with a glass of water followed by tea.

The making of *mishti* is an artform that has been perfected over centuries. *Mishti bhandars* (sweet shops) can be found at the end of the main streets in every neighbourhood and the selection is vast, each selling similar sweets but made to their own family recipes. Two of my closest friends, Piya and Debarun, who I often stay with in Kolkata, introduced me to several heritage sweetmakers in the city, such as Balaram's, Jugal's, Ganguram and Mithai. We never need an excuse to make a visit to these sweet *bhandars* and stand in front of the refrigerated counters filled with the most artistic sweets, imprinted with beautiful designs. The only difficulty is in choosing which beautiful treat to buy.

There are many different types of Bengali *mishti*: *sandesh* and *roshogolla* being two of the most popular, both made from milk. Milk features heavily in our sweets, be it fresh milk, condensed milk or milk solids. During the winter months, *nolen gur* (fresh jaggery drawn from the date palm tree) is a speciality in Kolkata, and different types of *sandesh* are made using this *gur*, which gives them an incredible taste. *Nolen gur* ice cream is one of the best ice creams I've ever had. The sweetness of the *gur* and little bits of *sandesh* in the cream make every mouthful simply divine! It's definitely a must-try if you visit Kolkata in winter.

Roshogolla are milk dumplings that are soaked in a sugar syrup and sold in clay pots in the sweet shops. In our house, these pots don't last long. We would take out a *roshogolla* with our fingers, squeeze out much of the syrup and then pop the whole thing in our mouths. In fact, some people have *roshogolla*-eating competitions for fun, to see who can eat the most *roshogolla* in one sitting. Among our friends, numbers have hit 45, which I find astonishing!

A plate of *sandesh*, glasses of water and cups of tea on the coffee table is a familiar sight in family homes in Kolkata. And for me, a meal is incomplete without having a sweet at the end, so I have very much enjoyed making the sweets in this chapter and reminiscing about the days when my parents would spend hours in the kitchen preparing these delicacies. I hope you enjoy making them and devouring them as much as we do in our household!

Sweet Set Yoghurt

MISHTI DOI

serves
10

Served in round clay pots of different sizes, this is a Bengali speciality found in all sweet shops and made in many homes. It is a sweet, slightly tangy, set curd that is served with other sweets on the side. In shops, this is sold unadorned, but at home we decorate it with dried rose petals when serving guests to make it look pretty. This recipe, which only uses three ingredients and is very easy, came from one of my mum's friends in London – she makes the most delicious Bengali sweets at home. Smooth in texture, this dish can easily be served on its own as a dessert to wow your guests.

1 x 400 g (14 oz) tin of evaporated milk

1 x 400 g (14 oz) tin of condensed milk

500 g (1 lb 2 oz) Greek-style yoghurt

dried rose petals, to serve (optional)

Preheat the oven to 200°C (400°F/ gas 6).

Place all the ingredients, except the rose petals, in a bowl and mix well with a hand blender.

Pour the mixture into an ovenproof dish, about 4 cm (1½ in) deep (the mixture can also be poured into small individual pots for single portions). Bake for 25 minutes if using one large dish or for 10 minutes if using individual pots.

Turn off the oven, but leave the yoghurt mixture in the warm oven for a further 20 minutes to set.

Carefully transfer to the fridge to cool and set further.

When ready to serve, remove from the fridge, decorate if you like, and divide among serving dishes.

Mango Pudding

AAM KHEER

serves
8

Aam kheer, also referred to as *aam payesh*, is a take on the classic Bengali dish *payesh*, which is a milk-based sweet dessert that is made all over India in different forms. The vast number of variations makes each one unique. In this dish, the milk is condensed over a flame for hours, until a thick custard-like consistency is achieved. *Payesh* can be made with just milk, or it can have rice or vermicelli added to it.

In our family, my dad makes *payesh* for us on our birthdays every year. It's a dish that is made for all special occasions. Being a summer baby, which is the season for mangoes, and since I loved them, my *payesh* was always *aam payesh*. The creaminess of the *kheer* with the sweetness of the mango makes a great dessert. Whenever we had birthday parties, I can remember there being a big pot of milk on the stove that was continuously stirred by mum or dad in order to achieve that perfect consistency. The important thing to remember is that this is a labour of love, and the continuous stirring of the milk makes the dish what it is.

750 ml (3 cups) full-fat milk
2 bay leaves
½ x 400 g (14 oz) tin of condensed milk
8 saffron strands
1 black cardamom pod

To decorate

8 tablespoons mango pulp
1 medium mango, peeled and cut into 1 cm (½ in) cubes
2 tablespoons almonds, finely chopped
saffron strands

Place a large heavy-based pot over a medium–low heat, pour in the full-fat milk and heat for about 10 minutes. After this time, very regular stirring needs to take place, otherwise the milk will burn at the bottom and spoil the *kheer*. Add the bay leaves and continue heating and stirring for a further 40 minutes.

Add the condensed milk and mix well, gently. After another 10–15 minutes, the milk will begin to condense. Add the saffron and black cardamom, continue heating and stirring regularly. The volume of milk will reduce substantially and begin to form into *kheer*. Once a thick consistency has been achieved, similar to custard, remove from the heat and allow to cool to room temperature.

Either dish the *kheer* into individual serving dishes and place in the fridge to chill or chill in the pot itself.

Once chilled, remove from the fridge just before serving and pour 1 tablespoon of mango pulp into the middle of each dish or portion. With a toothpick, swirl the pulp into any design. Add some chopped mangoes in the centre and sprinkle some sliced almonds and a couple of saffron strands on top. Be sure to decorate only just before serving.

Bengali Jaggery Curd Sweets

SONDESH

makes
20

With a soft, fudge-like consistency, *sondesh* are a Bengali sweet made from milk products. They can be made with *channa* (curdled milk, see page 178), but in this recipe I use ricotta, as I feel it gives a similar texture to the ones made in Kolkata. They are usually moulded into different shapes in wooden moulds, but if you don't have any moulds at home, I find the bottom of a pretty fluted drinking glass is just as effective to create an indented pattern. Popping the raisins in the middle of the *sondesh* was an activity I always shared with my sister, sitting at the dining table laughing and giggling, decorating the *sondesh* before they were refrigerated to be ready for our guests in the evening.

400 ml (1½ cups) evaporated milk

300 g (1⅓ cups) ricotta cheese

100 g (3½ oz) jaggery, crumbled into small pieces

2 tablespoons ghee

4 saffron strands

20 plump juicy raisins (optional)

1 handful of pistachios, very finely sliced (optional)

Place the evaporated milk and ricotta cheese in a saucepan and set over a medium heat. Mix together and reduce until the milk mixture has condensed and halved in quantity. Add the crumbled jaggery and stir until completely melted. Mix in the ghee and saffron, then remove from the heat and leave the mixture to cool and thicken slightly.

Divide the mixture into 20 equal portions. Form each one into a round ball, then flatten each ball in the palm of your hand and place on a plate.

If you like, you can imprint the tops of the *sondesh* with the bottom of a moulded glass or use a sweet mould to create a pretty pattern. Place a raisin and a few slices of pistachio in the middle of each *sondesh* and press gently to firm them in. Place in the fridge to set.

Serve at room temperature.

Milk Dumplings in Light Sugar Syrup

ROSHOGOLLA

serves
4

Roshogolla are one of the most popular Bengali sweets. They are dumplings made from curdled milk (this product is called *channa* and is similar to *paneer* – savoury dishes are made from it, too), which can be found soaking in sugar syrup in clay pots at all sweet shops. Using only a handful of ingredients, the dish is very simple. Other Bengali sweets incorporate *roshogolla*, such as *rasmalai*, which are *roshogolla* soaked in *malai* milk. Famous in Ballaram's (a well-known Kolkatan sweet shop) is the baked *roshogolla*, its crème brûlée-style topping is simply irresistible.

Roshogolla-eating competitions used to take place on the streets among sweet vendors. They were lots of fun and loved by many, although they are a fading tradition now because of the amount of sugar consumed in one go!

2 litres (8 cups) full-fat milk

2 tablespoons freshly squeezed lemon juice

For the syrup

500 ml (2 cups) water

100 g (scant ½ cup) white granulated sugar

3 green cardamom pods

To decorate

pinch of saffron strands

finely chopped pistachios

Heat the milk in a heavy-based pan over a medium heat. When the milk starts boiling, switch off the heat and pour in the lemon juice. Stir and the milk will immediately start to curdle. Lay a muslin (cheesecloth) carefully over a bowl large enough to contain all the milk, hanging the edges over the sides of the bowl. Pour the mixture onto the cloth, pick up the sides of the cloth and slowly squeeze it towards the middle, forming a ball of curds. Tie the muslin over the sink tap and leave to hang for 45 minutes. This allows the liquid to drain out.

Take the ball of *channa* from the muslin and place on a clean work surface. Firmly knead it for at least 8 minutes, pushing it into the counter with the heel of your hand to smooth out the paste, then bringing it back together, until it is fine and smooth in texture. Divide into 16 equal portions and form each into a perfectly round ball in your palms. Set aside.

Bring the water for the syrup to the boil in a large saucepan over a medium heat. Add the sugar and cardamom pods and bring the mixture to a gentle rolling simmer. Carefully add the *channa* balls to the syrup – do not overcrowd the pan with too many, as they will expand in size. Cover the pan and let them cook for 5 minutes. To ensure that no steam escapes from the lid, it can be carefully covered with a cloth for the duration of cooking. After 5 minutes, gently swirl the *roshogolla* with a spoon and cover for a further 3 minutes.

Remove from the heat and allow to cool in the pan, after which they can be served or chilled.

To serve, place a few *roshogolla* in each serving bowl, spoon over a couple of spoonfuls of the syrup and decorate each *roshogolla* with a couple of strands of saffron and some chopped pistachios.

Filled Sweet Pancakes

PATISHAPTA

For the crêpes

130 g (scant 1 cup) plain (all-purpose) flour

65 g (½ cup) fine semolina

½ teaspoon salt

400 ml (1⅔ cups) full-fat milk

rapeseed (canola) oil spray, for cooking

For the filling

2 tablespoons ghee

50 g (½ cup) fine desiccated (dried unsweetened shredded) coconut, plus extra to decorate (optional)

½ teaspoon ground cinnamon

1 teaspoon ground cardamom (ideally freshly ground)

3 tablespoons full-fat milk

2 tablespoons condensed milk

Although I have enjoyed these for many years, I only learned how to make them while writing this book. When I asked my mum about the recipe, she confidently asked me to call again in the evening when she would have the recipe for me. When I called home, I could hear laughing in the background and lots of action. My mother had called round a couple of her close friends and together they were making *patishapta*, with each assigned a specific role: one writing, one prepping and measuring, and the other cooking. It felt like an evening in Kolkata, where aunties spontaneously meet, have a catch up and often make these treats together. *Patishapta* fall under the category of *pitha* (batter pancakes or fritters), which are made using the seasonal harvest. There are several different types of *pitha* that can be made, commonly during *Poush Sankranti*, which marks the end of the winter months when prayers are made to the Sun God for a fruitful season of crops. *Patishapta pitha* is one of the most common types. They are very thin crêpes, filled with either a coconut filling, or *kheer* with jaggery. I've given you the coconut version here.

Start with the filling. Heat a shallow frying pan (skillet) over a medium heat and add the ghee. Once it has melted, add the coconut and fry for 2 minutes, then add the ground cinnamon and cardamom. Mix well and cook for a further 2 minutes. Add the milk, stir and bring to a gentle simmer, then add the condensed milk. Simmer for a further 2 minutes until the mixture is quite thick, then remove from the heat and set aside.

Combine the ingredients for the crêpes, except the oil for cooking, in a bowl. Whisk until the batter becomes thin and smooth.

Heat another frying pan over a medium heat. Spray with oil to lightly coat the base. When hot, spoon about 2 tablespoons of batter into the centre of the pan. Spread the batter evenly to make a circle about 13 cm (5 in) in diameter. Cook for about 1½ minutes, then take a tablespoon of the coconut filling mixture and lay in a straight line down the centre of the crêpe. Fold both sides of the crepe into the middle, then gently remove from the pan and place on a plate. Repeat with the rest of the batter and filling.

Place the *patishapta* on a serving dish or on individual plates. Serve warm, sprinkled with a little extra desiccated coconut, if you like.

Fennel Pancakes in Syrup

MALPUA

makes about **10** pancakes

Malpua are small round pancakes, crispy on the edges and soaked in a sugar syrup. Popular in North India, each state has their own way of making them, and they are enjoyed during festivities, *pujas* and weddings. Traditionally, the *malpua* batter would be deep-fried in ghee, then the pancakes soaked in syrup and served with a sweetened milk called *rabri*. Increasingly, they are made at home, but in a healthier way – yes, even sweet-loving Bengalis are seeking alternative ways of cooking! The pancakes are often infused with fennel and cardamom, and some regions even add nuts and fruits. We make this recipe regularly and it can be served as a dessert after dinner parties. In Kolkata, one of the ingredients used is *khoy* (milk solids). In this recipe, I use whole dried milk as a substitute, and the taste is very similar. Dipping the *malpuas* in the syrup is optional – they taste delicious just off the pan, too!

2 teaspoons fennel seeds

seeds from 1 green cardamom pod

150 g (1 cup) plain (all-purpose) flour

50 g (½ cup) whole milk powder

1 tablespoon ghee

2 tablespoons brown sugar

20 g (¼ cup) desiccated (dried shredded) coconut

2 tablespoons full-fat cottage cheese

¼ teaspoon baking powder

190 ml (¾ cup) lukewarm water

3 saffron strands

rapeseed (canola) oil, for shallow-frying

8 pistachios, finely sliced into thin strips, to decorate

dried rose petals, to decorate

For the syrup

120 ml (½ cup) water

1 black cardamom pod

3 cloves

120 g (½ cup) brown sugar

In a spice grinder, combine 1 teaspoon of the fennel seeds with the green cardamom seeds. Blitz to a fine powder.

In a mixing bowl, add the flour, milk powder, ghee, brown sugar, coconut, cottage cheese, baking powder, warm water and the remaining teaspoon of fennel seeds. Whisk (either by hand or using an electric mixer) to a thin batter. Finally, add the fennel and cardamom powder and the saffron. Fold in well so that the powder is fully mixed through.

Heat a splash of oil in a frying pan (skillet). When hot, add 2 tablespoons of the mixture to the pan to form a thin round pancake. They should be about 2 mm (¹⁄₁₆ in) thick and 12 cm (4¾ in) in diameter, so they can be turned easily. Cook on the first side for about 3 minutes until browned, then turn and cook the other side. You can cook 2–3 pancakes at any one time, but be sure not to overcrowd the pan. When cooked, remove to drain on kitchen paper. Repeat with the rest of the mixture.

To prepare the syrup, combine the water, black cardamom and cloves in a saucepan and bring to the boil. Skim out the spices, then add the sugar and keep stirring until the sugar has melted and you have a thin syrup. Switch off the heat, but ensure the syrup stays hot, otherwise it will begin to harden.

Have a serving dish ready to hand. With some tongs, take a *malpua* and dip it carefully into the syrup, then remove immediately and lay on the serving dish. Repeat with all the *malpuas*. Once they have been all laid on the serving dish, decorate with sliced pistachios and dried rose petals. Serve at room temperature.

Classic Places to Eat

Kolkata is often referred to as the best destination for gastronomic food in India. With its pot pourri of cultural influences, from the British Raj to Chinese immigrants and the Jewish community, a huge variety of distinctive dishes can be found in its restaurants, street food stalls and cafés. Here are just a handful of the places that I would strongly recommend you visit when in town, although there are so many other delights to be found!

Peter Cat

This restaurant opened on Park Street in 1975 and is one of Kolkata's older establishments. Famous for its *chelo kebab*, it has a regal feel with dimmed lighting and an intimate atmosphere.

Mocambo

Also in Park Street and with the same owner as Peter Cat, Mocambo is a fine dining restaurant known for steak and wine. Back in the 1970s, this restaurant was for the elite and was a popular jazz bar. It is famous for its devilled crab, which is baked with cheese and served in its shell.

Nahoum and Sons

Although the Jewish community is nearly extinct in Kolkata, this 115-year-old Jewish bakery based in the heart of New Market remains. Famous for their fruit cakes, this bakery with its original teakwood furniture and recipes that go back three generations has truly stood the test of time. The cakes and pastries are simply unique and at Christmas the queues for their Christmas cake are enormous, with people patiently waiting hours for their turn.

Maharaj

This no-frills, open-fronted shop serves the best breakfast in South Kolkata. *Radhabollobhi* and potato curry are served out of one side of the shop and freshly made *chai* is served on the other side.

Nizam's

Based in Hogg Street since 1932, this is where the *kathi roll* originated. This flaky *porota* cooked with an egg and filled with grilled chicken kebab, salads and green chutney with a dash of lime is an absolute must on any visit to Kolkata. Many variations are now available around the city, but Nizam's claims to be the original and best.

6 Ballygunge Place

A must-visit for classic Bengali delicacies. This 100-year-old white mansion on the street corner has been converted into a fine dining restaurant with a homely ambience. They are particularly famous for their *prawn malai* cooked and served in hollowed-out coconut shells.

Amber

Dating back to colonial times, this restaurant began its life as Central Hotel, my great grandfather's restaurant. After independence, it became Amber and specialised in North Indian cuisine. To this day, it holds a special place in many people's hearts and stomachs!

Arsalan

Famous for Mughlai cuisine, particularly their *biryanis*, which are cooked in massive pots called *dekchis*, the service at this restaurant is quite a treat. *Biryani* in Kolkata is famous for having potato in it – the soft yellow potatoes absorb the flavours of the whole spices and the meats during cooking, so there is always a fight for who gets a potato when it is being served out. Come here for the best *biryani* in town.

BREADS & RICE

no matter how tasty a main dish is, I feel it is incomplete without a portion of a rice dish or a flatbread. Both improve the experience of eating and really allow the taste of each individual dish to come through, enhancing rather than masking.

In Kolkata, fresh puffed *rooti* or *porota* that have been cooked in ghee will often be served. Many street-side shacks make *rooti* fresh in the evening, for customers to pick up on their way from work. One of my favourites is the *rumali rooti* (handkerchief roti). These are very thin, extra-large sheets of dough, that are cooked on top of an upside-down karai with a high flame under it. The way the dough is rolled out, then stretched out by hand into the thinnest of sheets is quite amazing.

As West Bengal is one of India's largest rice cultivators, rice is the most common staple in households. In fact, one of the most classic dishes that Bengalis are known for is *maach aar bhaat* (fish and rice). Our rice is cooked in so many different ways and Bengalis are quite fixed in their ways, only serving certain rice preparations with certain dishes. For example, the rice that would be served with a fish dish would usually be plain steamed rice (page 200), yet with *kosha mangsho* (lamb curry) either *mishti pilau* (sweet rice, page 201) or *ghee bhaat* (page 200) is served.

One thing I learned early when cooking rice is the importance of washing it properly. In our home, my dad would make the rice dishes when entertaining and I can remember him standing in front of the sink, washing the rice grains with so much attention and care. He always said that washing the grains properly was the secret to fluffy rice. Washing the rice thoroughly with your fingers a few times gently removes the starch from the rice, but care must be taken not to break the grains. I have always remembered this and it is a brilliant piece of advice for the perfect Indian rice every time!

Puffed Fried Breads

LUCHI (LOO-CHI)

serves 4
makes 20 luchis

A quintessential Bengali breakfast nearly always features *luchi*. These light golden, puffed breads are paired with different *torkari* and are a classic weekend breakfast in many households. Also, no festive meal is complete without them. The element that makes them Bengali is the sole use of maida (refined all-purpose flour) and no atta (unrefined flour).

I have fond memories of Sunday mornings in Kolkata, where our *ran-nar mashi* (cook aunty) used to come and make this fresh for us with a *shada torkari* (white potato curry) and *aachar* (pickles). Even now, whenever I go back to my parents' home, the thought of having *luchi* with a simple vegetable *torkari* is the most comforting feeling.

250 g (2 cups) plain (all-purpose) flour
½ teaspoon salt
½ teaspoon sugar
1 tablespoon ghee
1 tablespoon vegetable oil, plus extra for deep-frying and oiling
125 ml (½ cup) lukewarm water

Put the flour in a mixing bowl and make a well in the middle. Add the salt, sugar, ghee and oil, and mix with your hands for about 3 minutes until crumbly, ensuring the ghee has melted. Carefully add half of the water and begin to knead into a dough consistency. Keep adding the water a little at a time and kneading until a firm but bouncy dough is achieved. Form into a ball, cover with a damp dish towel and leave to rest in the bowl for 20 minutes.

On a clean work surface divide the dough into quarters. Each quarter should be divided into 5 equal balls, to achieve 20 balls in total. Roll each into an even sphere and set aside.

In a karai or wok, heat enough oil for deep-frying over a medium–high heat.

While the oil is heating, take each ball and flatten it to a disc with the palm of your hands. Very lightly oil the work surface and each disc of dough. Use a rolling pin and a long rolling action to roll the balls into discs about 10 cm (4 in) in diameter, lifting the dough and changing direction from time to time.

Check that the oil is hot enough by carefully placing one side of a *luchi* into the oil without letting go. If it starts to bubble, the oil is ready. Turn the heat to medium, then carefully place one *luchi* at a time into the oil. Cook for 1 minute on each side, allowing it to puff up and turning with a slotted spoon. Do not allow them to brown – *luchis* should be cream in colour. When the *luchi* has puffed up (note that not all will puff) or has cooked for 1 minute on each side, carefully remove and place on a plate lined with kitchen paper to drain.

Repeat until all the *luchis* are cooked. Serve immediately with your choice of *torkari* and/or *achaar*.

Lentil-Filled Puris

RADHABALLABHI

makes
15

Famous in Kolkata, this delicious lentil-filled puri has stolen many a Bengali heart. Served out of the front of shops, where they are made in batches of 20–30 at a time in enormous *karais*, the art of the well-practised system is amazing to watch. The speed at which the *radhaballabhis* are made is often the same speed at which they are sold! Served in *sal patha* (dried leaf) bowls, with a light gravied potato *torkari* and masala tea (both of which are usually being made alongside), it's a perfect breakfast combination. People gather round the stores and enjoy the freshly made dishes standing up. The owner of Maharaja, my favourite spot for these, got to know my family as regular customers. The morning banter while standing and eating was always something quite special.

This dish is a labour of love as it consists of a three-stage process, but it is most definitely worth it. I also love the beauty of eating them in *sal patha* bowls – eco-friendly, cheap and no washing up!

For the dough

500 g (4 cups) plain (all-purpose) flour, plus extra for dusting

½ teaspoon salt

1 tablespoon ghee

1 teaspoon carom seeds

lukewarm water, as needed

For the filling

175 g (scant 1 cup) white urid dal (split black gram), soaked overnight in water to cover by 2.5 cm (1 in), then drained well

3 green chillies, roughly chopped

2.5 cm (1 in) piece of fresh ginger, grated

1½ teaspoons fennel seeds

1 teaspoon cumin seeds

1 teaspoon salt

3 tablespoons water, or as needed

To cook the filling

2 tablespoons mustard oil or rapeseed (canola) oil

2 teaspoons nigella seeds

1½ teaspoons asafoetida

1½ teaspoons sugar

½ teaspoon salt

To finish

vegetable oil, for deep-frying

To make the dough, combine the flour and salt in a medium bowl, mixing well. Add the ghee, carom seeds and a small amount of lukewarm water. Keep mixing and adding water a very little at a time, until a soft dough is formed with no flour remaining on your hands or the sides of the bowl. Knead well, cover with a damp dish towel and leave to rest for 30 minutes.

To make the filling, place the drained dal in a blender along with the other filling ingredients and blend until thick and smooth.

To cook the filling, heat the oil in a medium karai or wok over a medium heat. Add the nigella seeds, taking care not to burn them. After 1 minute, carefully add the filling mixture (it will sizzle). Stir well for 3–4 minutes. Add the asafoetida, sugar and salt, and cook for about 10 minutes over a low–medium heat, stirring from time to time. The water should slowly evaporate and the mixture become a firm-ish dough consistency. Remove from the heat, place on a plate and allow to cool completely.

Meanwhile, on a flour-dusted work surface, divide the bread dough into 15 portions and form each into a ball.

Take a ball of dough and flatten with both palms, then make it thinner and larger by pressing the edges with your thumb and forefingers. Cup the dough in your palm and fill with 2 teaspoons of cooled dal filling. Pinch the edges of the dough to enclose the filling in a ball. Do the same for all 15 portions.

Wipe away any excess flour and lightly oil the work surface. With a rolling pin, roll out each ball into a flatbread about 13 cm (5 in) in diameter. Take care not to roll too much, otherwise the filling will start to spill out.

Heat a karai or wok with enough oil for deep-frying over a medium heat. To check that the oil is hot enough for frying, carefully lower one edge of a *radhaballabhi* into the oil. If it starts to bubble, the oil is ready and you can gently release the bread into the oil. Cook for 1½ minutes on each side, or until golden and puffed up. Remove with a slotted spoon and place on a plate lined with kitchen paper to drain. Repeat for all the flatbreads.

Serve warm with *Aloor Dom* (page 41) and *Elachi Cha* (cardamom-infused tea, page 160).

Flatbreads Stuffed with Spiced Potato

ALOO'R POROTA

makes
8

Aloo'r porota is probably the most popular type of stuffed flatbread in India. In many regions, they make up an important part of a meal. These are more rich and substantial than *rootis*, as they are kneaded with oil, stuffed with a filling and then cooked with butter. They are delicious piping hot, and can be eaten with a raita and pickle (see *Begun Achar* on page 216) as a meal in itself.

130 g (scant 1 cup) plain (all-purpose) flour, plus extra for dusting

130 g (scant 1 cup) chakki atta (wholemeal chapati) flour

1 teaspoon salt

½ teaspoon sugar

2 tablespoons rapeseed (canola) oil

170 ml (⅔ cup) warm water, or as needed

butter, for cooking

For the filling

4 potatoes, quartered

2 tablespoons rapeseed (canola) oil

1 teaspoon cumin seeds

1 teaspoon grated fresh ginger

2 green bird's eye chillies, finely chopped

1 teaspoon amchur (mango) powder

1 teaspoon chaat masala

1 teaspoon Jeera Bhaja Masala (page 218)

2 tablespoons chopped coriander (cilantro)

1½ teaspoons salt, or to taste

In a large mixing bowl, combine the flours, salt, sugar and 1 tablespoon of the oil. Mix gently with clean hands, then slowly add the lukewarm water a very little at a time with one hand and keep mixing with the other hand until it becomes a dough. Continue kneading in the bowl until the dough is soft and non-sticky. Form into a ball and coat with the remaining tablespoon of oil, then cover with a damp dish towel and leave to rest for 45 minutes.

Meanwhile, make the filling. Place the potatoes in a saucepan, cover with water and bring to the boil, then cook over a medium heat for about 7 minutes until they are soft to the point of a knife. Drain, then mash to a smooth consistency.

Heat the oil in a frying pan (skillet) over a medium heat, then add the cumin seeds. Once the aromas are released, add the mashed potatoes, along with the remaining filling ingredients and mix well with a wooden spoon, ensuring there are no lumps. Cook for a further 4 minutes until the mixture has dried out a little.

Transfer the filling mixture to a bowl and leave it to cool slightly. Wipe the pan clean and set aside.

Divide the rested dough into 8 balls. Flatten each ball to a palm-sized disc, then cup each piece in your hand and fill with 1½ tablespoons of the filling mixture. Pinch the edges of the dough together to enclose the filling and gently roll into a ball again. Repeat until all are filled.

On a flour-dusted work surface, carefully roll out a ball with a rolling pin to about 15–17 cm (6–7 in) in diameter and 2 mm (⅛ in) thick.

Heat ½ teaspoon of butter in the frying pan over a medium heat. Once melted, place the *porota* in the pan and cook for 2 minutes on each side, then remove to a plate lined with kitchen paper to absorb any moisture.

While each *porota* is cooking, roll out another in the same way, so it is ready to place in the pan as soon as the cooked one is removed. Add more butter to the pan as needed.

Serve hot.

Wholemeal Flatbreads

ROOTI

makes
15

Although Bengal's staple food is rice, flatbreads such as *rootis* have also become an integral part of our meals. The classic Bengali combination of *rooti* and *torkari* is well known throughout households in Kolkata. This versatile flatbread can be eaten at any time of day: at breakfast and dinner, but also for office and school lunches. Rolled in foil with a side of dry *torkari*, they make a perfect, filling packed lunch.

The sheer joy of making a *rooti* that puffs up like a balloon on top of the gas stove is very satisfying. In joint family households like my mother-in-law's, 120 *rootis* would be made every evening for the family of 14! Each of her brothers would eat 8–10 during their dinner.

300 g (2 cups) chakki atta (wholemeal chapati) flour, plus extra for dusting

1 teaspoon salt

230 ml (scant 1 cup) very warm water, or as needed (may vary slightly depending on the brand of flour used)

Combine the flour and the salt in a mixing bowl. Gradually add tiny amounts of water at a time, mixing by hand until there is enough water to bind the mixture together. Take care not to add too much water, otherwise the dough will become gloopy. Continue to knead the mixture by hand until a soft dough forms. Form into a ball, cover with a damp dish towel and leave to rest for 30 minutes.

Once rested, divide the dough into 15 balls of equal size. On a flour-dusted work surface, place another tablespoon of flour in a heap. Take each ball and flatten with your palm, dust one side of the ball on the pile of flour and place on the work surface. Flatten with your fingers, then begin to roll out with a rolling pin, lifting the dough from the work surface every few rolls, to avoid it sticking. Roll out to 15 cm (6 in) in diameter.

Heat a dry frying pan (skillet) over a medium heat for about 4 minutes until hot. If you are using a gas stove, place a *rooti* in the pan and cook for 2 minutes on each side, then remove the pan from the heat and place the *rooti* directly on the hob flame – it should begin to inflate. After 30 seconds, use tongs to turn the *rooti* and cook for a further 30 seconds, then remove immediately to a plate lined with kitchen paper to absorb excess moisture. If you are using an electric stove, just increase the cooking time to 4 minutes on each side. Repeat until all are cooked.

Once the *rootis* have been cooked, cover with foil to keep them hot.

Serve warm with a *torkari* (see page 36) and some salad.

Pea-Filled Flatbreads

MOTORSHUTIR KACHORI

When peas are in season, do use them fresh from their pods – they are so sweet. During the winter months in Kolkata, my dad would buy large, plump pods from the morning market and the childrens' job would be to sit and pop them open to strip them of the peas. We would do this sitting in the morning sun on the *chaath*, filling a woven basket with the sweet peas. They make a tasty filling for these deep-fried breads, which are traditionally served with *aloor dom* (page 41).

makes

15

For the dough

500 g (3⅓ cups) medium chapati flour

500 g (3⅓ cups) plain (all-purpose) flour, plus extra for dusting

½ teaspoon salt

2 teaspoons rapeseed (canola) oil

1 teaspoon ghee

lukewarm water, as needed

For the filling

500 g (generous 3 cups) peas (defrosted if frozen)

3.5 cm (1½ in) piece of fresh ginger, finely grated

½ chilli, finely chopped (optional)

½ teaspoon salt

1 tablespoon rapeseed (canola) oil, plus extra for deep-frying

1 teaspoon cumin seeds

1 teaspoon asafoetida

1 teaspoon Jeera Bhaja Masala (page 218)

To make the dough, combine the flours and salt in a medium bowl and mix well. Add the oil and ghee and a small amount of lukewarm water. Keep mixing and adding in the water a very little at a time until a soft dough is formed and no flour remains on your hands. After kneading well, place a damp dish towel over the dough and leave it to rest for at least 30 minutes.

To make the filling, place the peas, ginger, chilli (if using) and salt into a food processor. Blitz to a coarse texture (30 seconds usually does the trick).

Heat the tablespoon of oil in a medium frying pan (skillet) over a medium heat. When hot, add the cumin seeds. After 1 minute, add the pea mixture and sauté for about 5 minutes. Stir in the asafoetida and leave over the heat until the mixture has dried out and is just starting to become flaky. Remove from the heat and allow to cool.

Divide the dough into 15 portions and form each into a ball. Flatten one ball with your palms into a flat circle, then use your thumbs to press out the edges to make it thinner and larger. Cup it your palm, so the dough takes that shape, and fill with 2 teaspoons of the filling. Pinch the sides closed to enclose the filling. Repeat until all are filled.

Dust the work surface with some flour and roll each ball into a flatbread about 15 cm (6 in) in diameter. Take care not to roll too much, otherwise the filling may spill out. Repeat with all the balls.

Heat enough oil for deep-frying in a pan over a medium heat. When the oil is very hot, carefully lower a *kachori* into the oil. It should immediately start to bubble and rise to the top. Cook for 1 minute until light golden, then turn and cook the other side. Remove with a slotted spoon to drain on kitchen paper. Repeat until all the *kachoris* are cooked.

Serve hot.

Authentic White Rice

SHADA BHAAT

serves 4

Shada bhaat (white rice) is the staple food of West Bengal. Boasting acres and acres of paddy fields, about 150 different types of rice are cultivated in the region. The most common grain, consumed on a daily basis, is *shedo chal*, which are unpolished, parboiled grains that are easy to digest. Basmati, with its long aromatic grains, is the most well known worldwide, and is increasingly eaten in Bengali households these days.

There are so many different ways to cook rice, but I find this the easiest and the results are always beautifully fluffy grains. Depending on which brand of rice you buy, they all take different amount of times to cook, so it's very important to keep a watch and taste regularly.

250 g (9 oz/1¼ cups) Basmati rice

Put the rice in a saucepan and set under cold running water. Gently wash, running your fingers through the grains, taking care not to break them. The water will turn cloudy (this is the starch). Gently pour it away without losing the rice. Repeat the process 3–4 times until the water is nearly clear. Wash one final time, then top up the pan with fresh water to about 4 cm (1½ in) above the rice.

Set the pan over a medium heat and bring to the boil, then add 150 ml (⅔ cup) of cold water and bring back to the boil. Reduce the heat to medium–low, add a further 150 ml (⅔ cup) water and bring back to the boil. After 5 minutes, check a grain of rice to see whether it is cooked. It should be soft but not mushy.

As soon as the rice is cooked, drain in a colander immediately. Run the rice under cold water for 10 seconds – this stops the cooking process. Drain again, then return to the pan and cover until ready to serve. Covering the cooked rice allows the grains to become fluffy in the steam.

Basmati with Ghee

GHEE BHAAT

serves 3

A rich, beautifully aromatic rice dish, that is perfect as an accompaniment to most Indian dishes.

130g (⅔ cup) Basmati rice

1 tablespoon ghee

250 ml (1 cup) water

1 teaspoon salt

Place the rice in a saucepan that has a lid and wash thoroughly by hand a few times until the water runs clear. Fill the pan with fresh water to above the level of the rice. Set aside for 1 hour, then drain in a fine sieve (strainer).

Place the pan back over a medium heat and add the ghee. When the ghee has melted, add the drained rice and stir gently with a wooden spoon, ensuring the grains don't break. Fry the rice grains for 2 minutes, then add the measured water and salt. Bring to a gentle simmer, then cook for a further 5 minutes.

Remove from the heat and cover the pan securely with the lid. Leave to rest for at least 10 minutes before serving.

Sweet Rice with Rasins and Cashews

PILAU

serves 6

Bengali *pilau* is slightly different from *pilaus* in other parts of India – it is sweet and traditionally uses a type of rice called *gobindobhog,* which is short and slightly fatter than Basmati rice. Often referred to as *mishti pilau,* the dish is cooked with ghee and flavoured with raisins and cashews, making it rich in flavour and texture. It is served at many festive occasions, birthdays and celebrations, and often paired (perfectly) with *Kosha Mangsho* (see page 134). If you can get hold of *gobindobhog* rice, do substitute it for the more readily available Basmati I am using here.

260 g (1⅓ cups) Basmati rice

2 tablespoons ghee

3 tablespoons cashew nuts

2 heaped tablespoons golden raisins

2 bay leaves

10 cloves

1 cinnamon stick

8 green cardamom pods, lightly crushed

1 teaspoon salt

1 teaspoon sugar

6 saffron strands

520 ml (2 generous cups) water

Wash the rice thoroughly in a bowl at least 3 times until the water runs clear. Wash carefully to ensure the grains don't break in the process. Once the water runs clear, fill the bowl with fresh water to 3 cm (1 in) above the level of the rice and leave to soak for 1 hour.

Drain the rice and leave in the colander for another 10 minutes to drain any excess water.

Heat 1 tablespoon of the ghee in a heavy-based pot that has a lid over a medium heat. When hot, add the cashews and cook for 1 minute, then add the raisins. Stir gently and cook for 2 minutes until both the cashews and raisins look glazed and lightly browned. Remove with a slotted spoon to drain on kitchen paper.

Add the remaining tablespoon of ghee to the pot. When it has melted, add the bay leaves, cloves, cinnamon stick and cardamom. Allow the aromas to release, then add the drained rice and gently stir to coat the rice with the ghee. Cook for 3 minutes, then add the salt, sugar and saffron. Stir again and cook for 2 minutes. Add the water and bring to a gentle simmer, and cook for a further 6 minutes.

Add the fried cashews and raisins to the pot, then reduce the heat to low and cover the pot securely. Cook for 10 minutes.

Remove from the heat, but keep the lid on the pot for a further 15 minutes.

When you are ready to serve, remove the lid and transfer to a serving dish.

BENGALI ACCOMPANIMENTS & SPICES

This chapter contains some fresh and simple salads, perfect to accompany both main meals and snacks, and a variety of other essential accompaniments.

Chutneys (*chutney*) and pickles (*achaar*) are hugely popular in Bengali cuisine. Our chutneys are always consumed in a very particular way. Bengalis like to have a tangy, sweet and sour dish made of fruit at the end of their main meal. It is served with the mains and while it is sweet it is not the dessert, instead being similar to a palate cleanser. According to custom, only a couple of teaspoons of chutney will be taken once all the other main dishes have been eaten. In our community, my mother is famous for her chutneys. She can make a chutney pretty much out of any fruit, adding the right whole spices and chilli heat along with sugar. They are so good, it's difficult not to have seconds. The two fruit chutneys I have included in this chapter are her most popular ones – and my favourites.

In Kolkata, the pickle jars, sitting on high shelves in my grandmother's kitchen, were always worth the wait. I have vivid memories of eating fresh, piping hot *porota* with a teaspoon of a delicious *achaar*. I've shared our family recipe for eggplant pickle here – it will lift many a meal into something very special.

Kasundi – or Bengali mustard – is another traditional preparation from the region. Ideally matched with fish dishes, it is also a very common pairing with many street-food snacks.

Finally, I have also included four Bengali spice mixes (*moshla*). These preparations are regularly made fresh in most households and will give your cooking the authentic taste that is distinctly Kolkatan.

Fresh Tomato and Black Chickpea Salad

TOMATO AAR KALO CHANA SALAD

1 x 400 g (14 oz) tin of kala chana (black chickpeas), drained

1 small red onion, peeled and finely chopped

1 green bird's eye chilli, finely chopped

1 handful of coriander (cilantro) leaves, roughly chopped

2 tablespoons good-quality olive oil

1½ teaspoons chaat masala

juice of ½ lime

4 ripe tomatoes

salt, to taste

As a child, during our summer holidays in Kolkata, I remember having this as a mid-afternoon snack at my gran's place. This is something that would be rustled up within a matter of minutes and was born from a need to serve a dish unexpectedly with ingredients that were available in the kitchen to guests one evening. Since then, it's become a favourite and is often served with snacks or even as a refreshing salad for lunch.

Combine all the ingredients, except the tomatoes and salt, in a bowl.

Deseed the tomatoes, then dice the remaining tomato flesh. Add to the bowl and mix everything together well. Check for salt and adjust to taste.

Home Salad

BARIR

½ cucumber

4 Bombay/white onions, halved and thinly sliced

1 green chilli, finely chopped

juice of ½ lime

1 tablespoon good-quality olive oil

salt, to taste

A quick and easy salad that my dad made for us as we grew up. Saturdays would be one of the only days my dad got some time to cook, and since it was a passion for him the dishes were ones that took time and involved several stages of cooking. If my parents were not entertaining guests, just the four of us would be in for a feast. He would make different types of biryanis or lamb dishes and they were all delicious. Often, the salads were simple yet just the perfect accompaniment to these dishes. As we grew older, and could take more heat, the number of chillies in the salad went up, too! In this recipe, I've kept the heat level to medium.

Slice the cucumber thinly, place in a bowl and add the onions, green chilli, lime juice, oil and salt to taste. Mix gently so the onion separates into strands. Leave to rest for 5 minutes to allow the onions and cucumber to absorb the flavours and release a little water. Don't rest for too long, otherwise it will become soggy. Serve immediately.

Tomato and Prune Chutney

TOMATO AAR PRUNER CHUTNEY

serves
6

A sweet and tangy chutney to complete a Bengali meal. As mentioned on page 20, the order of dishes in a Bengali meal is really important. Just as at the start, when a bitter dish is often served as a palate cleanser, in the same way once a meal is complete, a sweet dish is served that is also little tart to cut through it. This isn't a dessert – that comes after – it is simply a small sweet dish to complete the main course. Usually, a couple of teaspoons per serving is the right portion.

4 tomatoes

1½ tablespoons rapeseed (canola) oil

1 teaspoon Paanch Phoron (page 218)

2 dried red chillies

3 tablespoons sugar

1 teaspoon salt

120 ml (scant ½ cup) water

8 dried pitted prunes

1 tablespoon raisins

½ teaspoon Jeera Bhaja Masala
    (page 218)

Wash tomatoes and cut in half, then remove the stalk by cutting a small V in each half. Cut each piece in half and then in half again.

Heat the oil in a karai or wok that has a lid over a medium heat. When hot, add the paanch phoron and the dried red chillies and allow the aromas to release. After 1 minute, add the tomatoes and stir. The tomatoes will begin to go soft. Add the sugar and salt, stir well and cover for about 5 minutes. The mixture will begin to

look like a thick pulp. Add the water and bring to a simmer again. Drop the prunes and the raisins into the rolling simmer, stir well, then reduce the heat to low, cover and cook for a further 10 minutes.

Remove from the heat and empty into a serving dish. Sprinkle the bhaja masala over the top and bring to room temperature before serving. The chutney can be eaten at room temperature, or even chilled from the fridge, if you wish.

Sweet and Sour Plum Chutney

PLUM'ER CHUTNEY

 serves 6

Plums, also known as *aloo bhukhara*, have always been a popular fruit in Bengali households. This chutney made with ripe plums and Medjool dates is a treat after a Bengali feast. *Aloo bhukhara* is available as a dried fruit too, which can also be used. In our household, my mother was always in charge of making chutneys when entertaining guests and chutneys were only made when entertaining and not as a regular part of our everyday meals. My sister and I would always look forward to the dinner, as we would be able to indulge in the treats without being called away to do some sort of chore before our guests arrived.

In the Bengali menu, chutneys are traditionally served with the mains, but taken last as a palate cleanser. As they are quite strong in flavour, a tablespoon is usually an adequate serving.

2 tablespoons rapeseed (canola) oil

1 bay leaf

2 dried red chillies

1 teaspoon nigella seeds

12 ripe plums, pitted and quartered

1 tablespoon golden raisins

12 Medjool dates, pitted and quartered lengthways

12 prunes, pitted

1 teaspoon salt

50 g (¼ cup) demerara sugar

½ teaspoon Jeera Bhaja Masala (page 218)

Heat the oil in a medium karai or wok that has a lid over a medium heat. After 1 minute, add the bay leaf, dried chillies and nigella seeds. When they begin to crackle, stir in the plums and cook for about 4 minutes. Add the golden raisins, dates and prunes, mix well and cook for 5 minutes, then reduce the heat to low, cover and cook for a further 10 minutes until the fruits become mushy and their liquid is released.

Stir in the salt and sugar, cook for a further 5 minutes, then increase the heat to medium and allow the chutney to bubble for another 5 minutes. Remove from the heat and sprinkle over the jeera bhaja masala, then cover and allow to cool.

Transfer the chutney to a serving bowl and serve at room temperature or chilled.

Mint Chutney

PUDINA CHUTNEY

Fresh herbs help cut through the oil in snacks. Although the ratio in this chutney is heavier in coriander (cilantro), this is still referred to as mint chutney. This recipe is from the *telewala* who stands at end the end of my grandparents' lane every day from 3 pm, serving everyone from the school children to the office workers coming back home. His chutney has an amazing taste.

1 bunch of coriander (cilantro), washed and roughly chopped, including stalks

50 g (2 oz) mint leaves, washed and roughly chopped, including stalks

5 garlic cloves

5 cm (2 in) piece of fresh ginger, peeled and roughly chopped

3 green bird's eye chillies, roughly chopped

juice of 2 lemons

1½ teaspoons black salt (*kala namak*)

½ teaspoon Jeera Bhaja Masala (page 218)

Put all the ingredients into a blender and blitz to a thick green paste. Blitz a few times to get a nice smooth consistency.

Serve the required amount and pour the remainder into an airtight container. Store in the fridge for up to 7 days.

Mustard Relish

KASUNDI

makes about **20** servings

Paired with fish frys and many other street food delights, this popular condiment is made from fermented mustard seeds. It is a pungent, thick sauce, and many refer to it as Bengali mustard. *Kasundi* also has probiotic properties. Traditionally, the paste is made by grinding the mustard seeds and other ingredients on a *shil nora,* but we use the food processor to get the thick paste consistency.

50 g (5 tablespoons) black mustard seeds

50 g (5 tablespoons) yellow mustard seeds

3 tablespoons apple cider vinegar

1 small raw mango, roughly chopped

2 green bird's eye chillies

2 tablespoons freshly squeezed lime juice

1 teaspoon ground turmeric

3.5 cm (1½ in) piece of fresh ginger, peeled and roughly chopped

2 teaspoons sugar

salt, to taste

Soak both the black and yellow mustard seeds in cold water overnight, or for a minimum of 1 hour.

After soaking, place the seeds, vinegar, chopped raw mango, chillies, lime juice, turmeric and ginger into a food processor. Blitz to a semi-coarse paste (similar to the consistency of wholegrain mustard). Add the sugar and salt according to taste.

Serve as a condiment, then put the remainder in a clean jar and store for up to 10 days in the fridge, to maintain the pungent taste.

Eggplant Pickle

BEGUN ACHAR

This is one of our family recipes that has been handed down for a few generations. I'm not quite sure how many, but I do remember my gran telling me that her mother used to have jars of this pickling away, and that she used to sneak into the kitchen larder and scoop out large amounts with a dry roti left over from the night before. This is quite an unusual pickle, but one packed with plenty of flavour and intense spices. Served with rotis and a salad, it makes a perfect lunch or snack. It is also divine served with simple potato dishes.

1 eggplant (aubergine), skin on, cut into 1 cm (½ in) cubes

½ teaspoon ground turmeric

½ teaspoon salt

4 tablespoons mustard oil

4 tablespoons rapeseed (canola) oil

4 teaspoons Paanch Phoron (page 218)

5 garlic cloves: 3 finely grated; 2 very thinly sliced

½ teaspoon chilli powder

½ teaspoon ground cumin

½ teaspoon ground coriander

2 green chillies, slit lengthways

2 tablespoons apple cider vinegar

2½ tablespooons brown sugar

2 teaspoons salt

Lay the eggplant cubes on a plate and sprinkle with the turmeric and salt. Mix with a spoon, then leave to rest for 30 minutes. Once rested, dab the cubes gently with kitchen paper so that the excess water is absorbed.

Heat the mustard oil in a medium karai or wok over a medium heat. Carefully add the eggplant and fry for about 4 minutes, stirring occasionally, until light brown. Remove with a slotted spoon to drain on kitchen paper. Take care not to remove too much oil from the pan.

Add the rapeseed oil to the pan and heat. Add the paanch phoron and let the aromas release, then add the finely grated garlic, chilli powder, cumin and coriander. Mix regularly, so nothing sticks and burns. After 1 minute, add the chillies and the thinly sliced garlic. Mix well before adding the vinegar, brown sugar and salt. Allow to bubble gently for 1 minute, then add the eggplant back to the pan and gently fold it in, making sure the cubes don't break up and become mushy. Remove from the heat and allow the *achar* to cool.

This is now ready to eat and to be stored in sterilised airtight jars (see page 223). Keep for up to 3 weeks in the fridge.

Useful Spice Mixes

Jeera Bhaja Masala

Jeera (cumin) is used a lot in Bengali cooking, both whole seeds and ground. We also dry-roast the seeds and grind them, for a deeper aroma and taste with a certain smokiness. Adding this bhaja masala at the end of cooking (sprinkled on top) brings another layer of flavour to dishes.

2 tablespoons cumin seeds

Heat a dry pan for 1 minute, add the cumin and dry-roast until the aromas are released. Take care not to burn. Remove from the heat and allow to cool. Once cooled, grind in a clean coffee grinder to a fine powder. Store in an airtight jar.

Barir Bhaja Masala

1 teaspoon cumin seeds

1 teaspoon fennel seeds

6 cloves

1 bay leaf

1 cinnamon stick

1 teaspoon fenugreek seeds

1 teaspoon coriander seeds

Heat a dry pan for 1 minute, add all the spices and dry-roast until the aromas are released. Take care not to burn. Remove from the heat and allow to cool, then grind in a clean coffee grinder to a fine powder. Store in an airtight jar.

Bengali Garam Masala

2 cinnamon sticks

seeds of 6 green cardamom pods

6 cloves

Crush the spices in a pestle and mortar or in a clean coffee grinder to a semi-coarse powder. Store in an airtight jar.

Bengali Paanch Phoron

Throughout India, different regions have their own variation of this whole spice mix. It's used as the base of a temper and holds magical aromas that elevate a dish. This is the mix that is most commonly used in Bengal and can be found in a silver spice pot in most kitchens. You can buy it in supermarkets, but making your own fresh mix is worth it.

1½ teaspoons mustard seeds (of choice)

1½ teaspoons fennel seeds

1½ teaspoons nigella seeds

1½ teaspoons fenugreek seeds

1½ teaspoons celery seeds (this can be replaced with cumin seeds)

Mix the spices in a clean, airtight container and use according to your recipe.

Index

To sterilise glass jars for preserving
Wash jars and lids in a dishwasher or in
plenty of hot, soapy water. Rinse
thoroughly, then place upside-down on a
baking sheet lined with baking paper and
dry for 10 minutes in an oven preheated to
180°C (350°F/gas 4). Handle with care.

Acknowledgements

'It takes a village to raise a child', and that goes for writing a book, too. The numerous people that have had an impact on my life have brought me to this path of writing my first cookbook. It has been an incredible journey and one that I hope is the first of many. The behind-the-scenes team for this book have been phenomenal, sharing the same vision to bring it to life. It's been such a pleasure to work with you all and my thanks are enormous.

Firstly, to Paul McNally at Smith Street Books in Australia and Emily Preece-Morrison in the UK, thank you for spotting my potential and believing in me, and for your patience. I feel very lucky to have you as my publisher and editor. Steven Joyce, a really big thank you for making the dishes look so good with your amazing photography, and for your and Rebecca's continuous advice and support. Tom Groves and Kane Hulse, for always helping and making the day run so smoothly. Ellie and Toni, thank you for recreating the dishes so wonderfully and feeding us such beautifully prepared food for lunch. Hannah, the prop selection really felt as though they had been brought from Kolkata, thank you for your attention to detail. And to Georgie, thank you for the great design.

Without my parents, Ron and Rita, the majority of this book wouldn't exist. It is to your dedication and attitude to life and food that I am indebted and that I am eternally grateful for. The path of food that flows through our family generations is a beautiful story. Creating this collection of recipes that had to be cooked, tested, re-tested and written down precisely, often with several repetitions, tested your patience I know, but in the end we produced a book of exact, workable recipes that will now be available to a much wider audience to appreciate. This book is a celebration of Kolkatan recipes, the way you were taught to cook, that now we all can cook. Thank you.

Thanks to my sister Tania for being my sounding board and occasional co-tester (and selfie-taker). And to Piya, Debarun and Shaheb, for being at the end of the phone, no matter what time it was in Kolkata and how busy you were, for giving me advice and support throughout writing this book.

I would like to give a special mention to Arati mum, Jui, Manidipa Aunty and Ratna Aunty, for sharing some of their recipes.

Finally, to my husband Neelan and my girls. Having a baby while writing a book wasn't something I ever imagined would happen, but with your support, it became possible. Thank you for being my pillar of strength.

Additional picture credits

p.8 Aditya Prakash/Unsplash; pp.10–11 Sohan Rayguru/Unsplash; p.13 Dibakar Roy/Pexels; p.14 Rudra Chakraborty/Unsplash; p.17 Chiranjeeb Mitra/Unsplash; pp.18–19 Sauvik Bose/Unsplash; p.21 Subrata Deb/Pexels; p.23 Dibakar Roy/Pexels; p.27 Amandeep Singh/Unsplash; p.45 Ashwini Chaudhary/Unsplash; p.62 Dibakar Roy/Pexels; p.63 Dibakar Roy/Pexels; p.68 Ujjwal Jajoo/Unsplash; p.74 Neelan and Rinku Dutt; p.75 Neelan and Rinku Dutt; p.79 Arnab Dey/Unsplash; p.92 Rupinder Singh/Unsplash; p.93 Akash Gurle/Unsplash; p.101 Neosiam/Pexels; p.105 Martin Jernberg/Unsplash; p.109 Rudra Chakraborty/Unsplash; p.118 Shootcase Chronicles/Pexels; p.119 Sushmita Nag/Unsplash; p.128 Subrata Deb/Pexels; p.129 Rupinder Singh/Unsplash; p.133 Debashis RC Biswas/Unsplash; p.143 Sukanya Basu/Unsplash; pp.144–5 Dibakar Roy/Pexels; p.159 Rupinder Singh/Unsplash; p.171 Sandip Roy/Unsplash; pp.180–1 Heera Ramesh/Unsplash; p.187 Shivansh Upadhyay/Unsplash; p.191 Rahul Pandit/Pexels; pp.202–3 Dibakar Roy/Pexels; p.207 Vivek/Pexels.

Smith Street Books

Published in 2022 by Smith Street Books
Naarm | Melbourne | Australia
smithstreetbooks.com

ISBN: 978-1-92241-792-3

Publisher: Emily Preece-Morrison
Designer: Georgie Hewitt
Photographer: Steven Joyce
Food stylist: Ellie Mulligan
Prop stylist: Hannah Wilkinson
Proofreader: Vicky Orchard
Indexer: Vanessa Bird

Printed & bound in China by C&C Offset Printing Co., Ltd.

Book 226
10 9 8 7 6 5 4 3 2 1

FSC MIX Paper from responsible sources FSC® C008047